GEORGE LUNN

The 1912 Socialist Victory in Schenectady

GEORGE LUNN

The 1912 Socialist Victory in Schenectady

Bill Buell

Book design by Jessika Hazelton
The Troy Book Makers • Troy, New York • thetroybookmakers.com
Printed in the United States of America

To order additional copies of this title,
contact your favorite local bookstore
or visit www.shoptbmbooks.com

ISBN: 978-1-61468-518-0

ACKNOWLEDGEMENTS

Sometime before he passed away in 2004, Schenectady County historian Larry Hart told me about the time Schenectady elected a Socialist mayor in 1911.

I had seen a photograph of George R. Lunn in one of Hart's history books, and during a chance meeting at the Schenectady Gazette one Saturday morning – I was lucky enough to call him a colleague and a friend – I asked him to share some thoughts with me about the man who was not only a Socialist mayor, but also pastor at the First Reformed Church of Schenectady, a U.S. Congressman and Lieutenant Governor of New York.

Without Larry Hart and his Schenectady history books, I really don't think I would have ever started this project. I owe him a huge debt of gratitude, as do all local historians dealing with Schenectady's late 19th and early 20th century history.

But while it is true there were plenty of books used to put this work together, it truly is a product of newspapers. The microfilm collections at the Daily Gazette, the Schenectady County Public Library, the Schenectady County Historical Society, the Albany Public Library and the New York State Library were invaluable, as were visits to the Little Falls Historical Society Museum and the Herkimer County Historical Society. Also, I had the opportunity to look at the actual bound volumes of the Schenectady Gazette for both 1911 and 1912, for which I will forever be grateful. Looking at old newspapers page by page, instead of on microfilm, is a much more enjoyable experience.

There are also many people to thank for their help and contributions to this book. Former Gazette copy editor and friend Paul Girsdansky never saw the finish product, sadly, but his proofreading, suggestions and encouragement kept me going. City of Schenectady Historian Chris Leonard also gave the book a good read, as did several other local history buffs whom I hold in high esteem, including Frank Taormina and George Wise.

Daniel Carlson, associate pastor at the First Reformed Church in Schenectady, offered his input, as did my wife, Sarah Howes, a member at First Reformed, and Susan Hale, a friend who made sure I got all my Edward Everett Hale references correct. The staff and volunteers at the Grems-Doolittle Library at the Schenectady County Historical Society also willingly offered their help. Three different librarians at SCHS have helped with this project, including Michael Maloney and his two predecessors, Melissa Tacke and Katherine Chansky. My thanks go out to all of them.

Finally, I want to thank George R. Lunn for living the kind of life that made me think, "somebody's got to write a book about this man."

CONTENTS

INTRODUCTION

George Lunn, pastor, politician and public servant, lived 75 years, but it seems much longer. He was born in 1873, less than a decade after the Civil War, and he died in 1948, three years after America saved the world from fascism. During his life, horses were replaced by automobiles and man learned how to fly. Some people were still heading west by covered wagon when he was born - the trip took months - and by the time he died they were taking planes from New York to Los Angeles in just a few hours.

You could argue that the technological advances witnessed during Lunn's life were probably more significant than any other 75-year period in world history. What would interest him more, however, would be the social changes that occurred during that same span. From the excesses of the Gilded Age over the second half of the 19th century, to the prosperity and optimism of post World War II-America, the standard of living improved dramatically for the average citizen. Sixty-hour work weeks were outlawed, some Americans were actually enjoying two weeks of paid vacation, and a large middle class was developing. There were problems to be sure, but hope and opportunity seemed available to most everyone.

Lunn began his adult life concerned about the souls of men and women, but by 1912 his focus on the hereafter had changed to the here and now. As a minister and then a mayor, congressman, lieutenant governor and public service commissioner, Lunn worked tirelessly to make the world a better place for everyone.

1912 was the high-water mark for American Socialism, and as the year came to end, Lunn and his political career seemed destined for national prominence. But while the year ahead held so much promise for Lunn and the Socialist Party, neither saw what was coming. Socialist leader and presidential candidate Eugene Debs got 6 percent of the vote in 1912, his best effort in four tries at the oval office, but by 1919 he was in an Atlanta prison having been labeled a traitor by Woodrow Wilson. Lunn, meanwhile, left the Socialists in 1916, became a Democrat and won election to the U.S. House of Representatives. But his political roots - his earlier devotion to socialism and denunciation of capitalism - prevented him from climbing too high in the political arena, leaving aspirations of the governor's office and a U.S. Senate seat unfulfilled. This book will examine Lunn, Schenectady, N.Y., and the Socialist experience of 1912 as well as its roots and aftermath.

CHAPTER 1

A Confrontation

Most everyone recognized the good-looking, well-dressed gentleman walking toward the Front Street entrance of the American Locomotive Company in Schenectady, New York that Wednesday morning. The striking workers knew him, but Harry Bowen, captain of the company's guards and hired by the ALCO bosses to keep order, did not.

At around 6:45 a.m., January 3, 1912, George R. Lunn, a pastor-turned-politician beginning his third day as mayor of Schenectady, visited the plant to check on reports that paid company policemen had been swinging billy clubs as they paraded up and down Nott Street just outside the grounds of the city's second largest industry. It seemed an obvious ploy to intimidate the striking workers, and as far as Lunn was concerned it was not only immoral behavior, it was illegal.

Elected mayor as a member of the Socialist Party on November 11, 1911, Lunn had been the senior minister at the First Reformed Church of Schenectady from 1904-1909. Drafted by the city's Socialist local as their mayoral candidate, Lunn was swept into office by a wide margin over both his Democratic and Republican opponents. After reveling in his success and accepting congratulations from all over the country, including a wire from Socialist presidential candidate Eugene Debs, it was now Lunn's third day in office and time for the new mayor to get to work. Accompanied by one of the striking workers, a loud and boisterous member of the Boilermaker's Union named Barney Rafferty, Lunn marched up to the Front Street entrance, approached two armed guards and started asking questions.

"How many of you are on duty?" Lunn wanted to know.

"Around 30," one of them replied.

The other man wasn't so helpful.

"I don't see how it's any of your business," he said to Lunn.

As Lunn replied that he was just looking for information, Captain Bowen walked onto the scene and demanded to know what was going on. He confronted Lunn and informed him that he was on ALCO property and that if he didn't leave, the captain would throw him off the Front Street bridge into the Erie Canal.

This didn't sit too well with Rafferty, a Carrie Street resident in the city's Goose Hill section and a staunch Socialist who seemed to always be looking for a tussle, either verbal or physical. With things approaching a boil, a handful of uniformed city policemen, led by Sergeant John H. Bath of the 1st Precinct, showed up and immediately saluted Lunn, defusing the situation and forcing Captain Bowen to retreat back within the ALCO grounds after discovering his unknown visitor was Schenectady's newly-elected mayor.

"Yes, Captain Bowen did threaten to throw me off the bridge at the locomotive works this morning," Lunn told reporters later. "He did not know me, and I am glad he did not. He and his deputies undoubtedly treated me just as they have been treating workingmen and others who have had the temerity to approach the place. I certainly found out the treatment a workingman would receive from them if he dared to ask a legitimate question."

The next day the New York Times reported Lunn had actually assaulted Bowen, who in turn had demanded Lunn's arrest. The mayor said there was no physical confrontation, and local newspaper accounts also differed from the Times's inflammatory version of the incident.

"I had no real altercation with Captain Bowen," Lunn said. "None was necessary. I do not believe in, and will not tolerate violence. Besides, the city police were near at hand and I do not think I was in any danger, even from Captain Bowen."

Lunn joked that if Bowen had thrown him off the bridge, he would have felt "at home, that is, on city property," for he would have landed in the Erie Canal. Then, turning more serious, Lunn told reporters, "I was at the works to learn by personal investigation if deputy sheriffs and the company's special watchmen were patrolling the public streets with police clubs. They have no right outside the company's property, and they will not be allowed to patrol the streets of Schenectady in the manner reported. Our local police department is efficient and will give proper protection to every good citizen – the same to the workingman as to the employer. I saw a few strikers standing around the plant, but they were a quiet, well-behaved, entirely peaceable lot of men. I should guess there were about 75 of them."

Lunn added that his administration "wants to be fair with all regarding the enforcing of the law," and that he "shall allow no special privilege to any class with regard to this enforcement. We shall insist that the strikers have their rights fully protected, and we shall insist also that they obey the law. And we shall insist with equal vigor that the American Locomotive Company obey the law also."

Within two weeks the strike was over, but it was hardly a great victory for the workers. ALCO, citing decreased production, failed to hire back many of the strikers. For Schenectady's new Socialist mayor it was only a start, a small first step toward improving living and working conditions in the city, but a somewhat dramatic beginning to a 30-year career in public service.

CHAPTER 2

Schenectady

In the first decade of the 20th century, Schenectady was a boom-town. In 1886, however, when Thomas Edison decided to bring his Edison Electrical Works to the city, it had a population of just 14,000. Much of the male population worked at the Schenectady Locomotive Works upon Edison's arrival, but by 1892, when Edison's company merged with the Thomson-Houston Electrical Company, the newly formed General Electric Company quickly became the biggest industry in town. The locomotive works, meanwhile, while not matching GE's number of employees, also got much bigger in 1901 when it merged with seven other locomotive builders from around the East coast to form the American Locomotive Company. By 1910, those new workers helped Schenectady's population grow to nearly 80,000.

Immigrants flowed into the city looking for jobs and found them, but the injustices and class conflicts of the Gilded Age that were so prevalent in major metropolitan areas a few decades earlier now descended upon smaller American cities like Schenectady. New homes were built as the city expanded eastward away from the Mohawk River up State Street, Broadway, Eastern Avenue and Union Street. New roads needed to be paved, and new schools and churches built to accommodate Schenectady's new population. In such an environment there was money to be made and in Schenectady, as in other cities, many of the most powerful politicians were also its most successful businessmen, making things ripe for corruption. The Progressive Era, generally recognized as the time between 1890 and 1920, was all about addressing rampant political corruption, but national movements require their dynamic local leaders to really take root. In Schenectady, that individual was Lunn. His decision to shift the focus of his life to politics and away from the pulpit, accept the Socialist nomination on September. 27, 1911, and then his subsequent election, were events that undeniably changed life in Schenectady for the better.

Founded in 1661 by Dutchman Arendt Van Curler, Schenectady is one of the oldest inland cities on the North American continent, and for much of the 17th and 18th century the western frontier began just outside its stockade walls. The town survived a massacre by the French and Indians on February 8, 1690, and 100 years later was a small but thriving boat-building community on the southern bank of the Mohawk River. Although a large fire in 1819 destroyed many businesses along the Binnekill, a branch of the Mohawk that hugged Schenectady's western shoreline, it was that geographic location – its access to a navigable waterway – that gave the city such a bright future. The railroad and the steam locomotive secured that future. Schenectady, incorporated as a city in 1798, wouldn't become just another small town along the Erie Canal.

Just six years after the canal opened in 1825, the DeWitt Clinton, a steam locomotive named after the former New York governor, made its initial trek from Albany to Schenectady in the late summer of 1831. The Mohawk-Hudson Railroad, the brainchild of Stephen Van Rensselaer and George Featherstonhaugh, was born, and was one of the first in the country to provide both passenger and freight traffic. It was no coincidence that the Schenectady Locomotive Works, under the guidance of John Ellis and his four sons, became the country's leading manufacturers of steam locomotives. Still, despite the success of the railroad industry in Schenectady, the city had just 13,655 people according to the 1880 census. In 1890, the continuing success of the Schenectady Locomotive Works and the arrival of Edison's Electrical Works in 1886 helped that number jump to 19,902. In 1900, the census count was 31,682, and by 1910, with both the General Electric Company and ALCO in full production mode, Schenectady's numbers ballooned to 78,826, more than doubling the size of the city in 10 short years.

While most cities around the state were seeing population increases, nowhere did the figures compare with Schenectady. In Albany, the increase in population was minimal – 94,151 in 1900 to 100,253 in 1910. Over the same stretch, Utica went from 56,383 to 74,419, Syracuse from 108,374 to 137,249, Rochester from 162,608 to 218,149 and Buffalo from 352,387 to 423,715. Yonkers' jump of 65.5 percent in those 10 years (47,931 to 79,803) was a distant second to Schenectady's unparalleled increase of 129.9 percent.

Another measure of growth was the number of city streets, which was also increasing rapidly. There were 140 named streets in the 1890 Schenectady directory, and by 1900 that number increased to 326. In the ten-year stretch between 1900 and 1910, Schenectady added another 163 street names.

Many of the new people flooding into the city weren't the Dutch, English, Scots or Germans that had occupied upstate New York since the Colonial era. Instead, they were Italians and Poles looking for a better way of life than what Europe offered. In 1890, there were 220 foreign-born Italians living in Schenectady, and 196 foreign-born Poles. Twenty years later, in 1910, there were 3,660 foreign-born Italians in the city and 4,221 Poles. Schenectady's entire foreign-born population had increased to 18,631, or 24 percent of the total. Five years earlier, in 1905, the Schenectady County Historical Society was formed in order to celebrate and preserve the area's treasured history, but also as a direct response to the wave of immigration that many felt threatened its cultural legacy.

CHAPTER 3

Early Life

Lunn was born June 23, 1873 on a farm in Taylor County, Iowa, in the southeast part of the state. His parents were Martin Adolphus Lunn and Martha (Mattie) Bratton, and both of their fathers were farmers in Iowa within Taylor County. George Richard Lunn, Lunn's grandfather, emigrated from Lincolnshire, England and settled in the Cleveland area before moving to Iowa in the 1840s. His grandson, however, was never concerned about his family tree. While in Schenectady, Lunn wrote, "pride of ancestry never possessed my soul."

The nearest town to the Lunn farm was Lenox, a small village with an unpaved main street and a few houses and other buildings. The village wasn't incorporated until 1875 when the Creston to St. Joseph branch of the Chicago, Burlington and Quincy Railroad was completed.

In his unfinished autobiography, Lunn said the death of the family physician, Dr. N.S. Hornaday, and the assassination of U.S. President James A. Garfield, both in 1881, affected him greatly as a young boy. However, the idea of heaven that his Presbyterian parents had instilled in him meant that both men were in a much better place. He didn't read "Uncle Tom's Cabin" while growing up, but he did see a stage version, understanding the title character's death to be "a gateway whereby we reach that delectable place" called heaven, as he later wrote.

While three Lunn children died in infancy, George grew up with three brothers and two sisters. The family attended the United Presbyterian Church, a rather pious and reverential place according to Lunn's recollections. While he appreciated his religious upbringing, he didn't understand why Sundays had to be so solemn. When his grandmother admonished him for whistling on the Sabbath, Lunn was incredulous. More than three decades later as mayor of Schenectady he declared that the city's parks and movie houses could remain open on Sunday.

When George was 10, the family moved to Des Moines, Iowa. His father was in the real estate business, and had been hired to produce a listing of bankers, lawyers and real estate agents that would cover the entire U.S. Seven years into the project, his directory and all his notes were destroyed in a fire. With the family struggling financially as a result of the loss, George quit school in the eighth grade at the age of 12 and went to work selling newspapers on the streets of Des Moines. By the time he was 17 he was driving a horse-powered delivery wagon in South Omaha, Nebraska. He also decided to go back to school, finishing his high school requirements in three years before attending Bellevue College in Omaha for the next four years, graduating in 1897.

Lunn, who earlier had decided he wanted to become a minister, worked at various jobs – librarian, wood cutter, potato picker and dishwasher - to get through college, and also had begun preaching sermons. He got his start at a small church in Platte, a few miles west of Omaha, then went to a Presbyterian church in Craig, just north of Omaha, before moving to a larger Presbyterian church in nearby Lyons.

His sometimes-rebellious nature revealed itself at Bellevue College, an institution controlled by the Presbyterian Synod of Nebraska. Despite knowing it would cause him some trouble with school officials, Lunn couldn't resist going to see Alexander Salvini, a noted Shakespearan actor of the day, in a production of "Hamlet" at the South Omaha Theater. It was a Sunday. Writing that, "it was always a part of my nature to rebel against what I felt was unreasonable practice," Lunn wasn't contrite when he was called before the faculty the next day. Instead, he informed them that if he had another opportunity to hear Salvini he would do it, regardless of the day or whatever punishment he might face. "I can't recall," wrote Lunn, "that the rule ever changed, but I wasn't dismissed, either."

During this time, Lunn became a teacher and acting principal at a small school in Craig, Nebraska. He was encouraged by the

Republican party to run for superintendant in May of 1897, but declined. Instead, he headed to Princeton Seminary that fall.

On February 15, 1898, as Lunn was nearing completion of his first year in New Jersey, the USS Battleship Maine exploded, presumed to be the work of Spain, and sank in Havana Harbor. Although U.S. President William McKinley was at first opposed to any military confrontation, he relented and supported Congress's Declaration of War on April 11. The Spanish-American War was on, and while Lunn was initially uncomfortable with the conflict, he, like McKinley, had a change of heart. Back in Omaha for the summer to preach at the Presbyterian church there, Lunn watched the 3rd Nebraska – William Jennings Bryan's regiment – during some marching exercises and felt compelled to join up. He refused a commission as chaplain and instead was inducted into the army as a corporal.

Bryan's regiment never got out of Florida, but one officer and 31 enlisted men all succumbed to a form of malaria. Lunn himself got sick but soon recovered. His brother Thomas wasn't so fortunate. Two years younger than George, Thomas had attended the University of Nebraska, and was intending to enter Princeton Theological Seminary when he volunteered for the 2nd Nebraska Infantry. The two brothers crossed paths in Chickamauga, Tennessee, in July on their way to Florida, but two months later, on September 25, Thomas, a corporal, died of typhoid fever.

"If ever there was a saint on Earth, he certainly was a saint," wrote George Lunn following his brother's death.

The war was short, with hostilities ending on August 12 that same year. Lunn was back at school in the fall of 1898, but not at Princeton. Finding the faculty and the curriculum there a little too "ultra-orthodox," Lunn enrolled at Union Theological Seminary in New York City.

UTS was created by a group of Presbyterian churches in New York City in 1836. It was liberal from its inception and welcomed students from all backgrounds, a surprisingly ecumenical approach for the time. As forward-thinking as it was, however, UTS was still controlled by the General Assembly of the Presbyterian Church, which had veto power over all faculty appointments. That changed in 1893 after the general assembly first suspended and then expelled Rev. Charles Augusts Briggs for publicly stating that errors may have existed in the original text of the Holy Scripture, and that "reason and the church are each a fountain of authority which apart from Holy Scripture may and does savingly enlighten men." A University of Virginia alumnus and one of UTS's most outspoken professors, Briggs also argued that there was plenty of messianic prophecy that was not and could not be fulfilled. He also felt that Moses and Isaiah were not the prolific writers of biblical scripture they were made out to be. This kind of critical analysis of the Bible was not what the Presbyterians expected from their faculty, and while they successfully removed Briggs from the school, Union's administration responded by rewriting some of the school's regulations and declared that the church's governing body no longer had veto power on its faculty appointments. It was the beginning of a complete break from the authority of the Presbyterian Church, and it was into this boiling pot of anti-fundamentalist thought that Lunn entered in the fall of 1898. Also, in 1897, Briggs' daughter, Emily Grace Briggs, became the first female student to graduate from UTS. This may have stretched credulity as far as traditionalists were concerned, and Lunn's grandmother might have been one of them. George, however, felt right at home.

The spring of 1901 was an important time for Lunn. Along with graduating from UTS, he married Miss Mabel Healy on May 10, honeymooned in Europe, and accepted a summer position pastoring in Cold Spring, about 50 miles north of New York City on the Hudson River.

By 1902, Lunn was an associate pastor at the Lafayette Avenue Presbyterian Church in Brooklyn, and was "burdened with a perpetually disturbed conscience and in the thought that I as a minister and the church as an organization was failing to get at the roots of the great social wrongs."

Not everyone, however, felt like Lunn. In Schenectady, "The Committee of 13" was formed in December of that same year with the precise goal to "protect business interests from assaults by organized labor." These men, as did many members of the wealthy and middle class at that time, felt strongly that labor unions were a direct threat to capitalism. Three of the 13 men on the committee had close ties to the First Reformed Church, including Dr. Andrew Van Vranken Raymond, who had served both as pastor at First Reformed (1899-1901) and president of Union College (1894-1907), also in Schenectady.

The church closed out the 19th century with two of its most beloved pastors: William Elliot Griffis (1877-1886) and Albert C. Sewell (1886-1899). Griffis' pastorate was dominated by an emphasis on missionary work and an increased role for women in the church, and Sewell continued to stress those areas as well as following Griffis' practice of using a large consistory and committee system. He also started up the Christian Endeavor Society, designed to "promote an earnest Christian life," among its members, and began printing a church newspaper called "The Messenger."

Griffis was born in Philadelphia in 1843, and saw plenty of action with the 44th Pennsylvania Regiment during the Civil War. That service put his college experience on hold, but in 1869 he graduated from Rutgers and immediately sailed to Europe and then Japan. He worked as a physics professor at the Imperial University in Tokyo and wrote his first of four books on Japan before returning to the U.S. where he began pursuing a seminary degree, first at New Brunswick Seminary and then Union Theological Seminary. He graduated from UTS in 1877, and in the spring of that year was travelling around the Northeast, giving lectures on Japan. When a group of women from the First Reformed in Schenectady travelled to the Knox Reformed Church in the Helderbergs just west of Albany to hear Griffis speak, they were quite enamored with him. One of the group, a Miss Annie Boardman, submitted his name as a candidate for their pastorate to replace Dr. Ashbel Vermilye, who was leaving for Belgium after seven years in Schenectady. Griffis not only wowed the women. After being invited to speak at First Reformed on April 22, 1877, a week later the 33-year-old son of a sea captain and coal trader was offered his very first pastorate when the congregation agreed unanimously that he should be its next pastor. Griffis accepted and on May 31 left New York City to make Schenectady his new home. He enjoyed 10 happy years at First Reformed and married a Schenectady woman, Katherine Stanton, before continuing his ministerial and writing career in Boston and then Ithaca. He died in 1928 at the age of 84.

Sewall, meanwhile, came to Schenectady by way of Chesterville, Maine, Granville, New York, and Williamstown, Massachusetts. The youngest of 15 siblings, Sewall had three brothers that were ministers as was his father, Jotham Sewall, who was prominent enough in Maine to be referred to simply as "Father Sewall" or "The Apostle of Maine." Albert C. Sewall was ordained in 1871 through Williams College and the Congregational Church of Massachusetts, and remained at a Congregational pastorate in Williamstown, Mass., before being called to replace Griffis in Schenectady in 1886.

Sewall showed a strong interest in public education, and also was a supporter of the Spanish-American War, encouraging American aggression in Cuba during a sermon in May of 1898. By 1899, however, Sewall, then just 54, resigned from his position. "The years which we have spent together have been the most arduous of my life," Sewall wrote in his letter of resignation. "It has more than once seemed to me that I could no longer endure the strain incident to the faithful discharge of the duties of this position."

Just how Griffis or Sewall would have incorporated their pastorate into the changing scene in Schenectady at the dawn of the 20th century we can't say. Raymond's work on the Committee of 13 at the turn of the century made it clear where his sympathies were, although, while at First Reformed his position there was always listed as interim. While he was not one of First Reformed's more memorable ministers, he is generally regarded as a very successful president of Union College, having reversed that institution's sinking fortunes during his 13 years at the helm. In 1901 his successor at First Reformed, John S. Zelie, put most of his energy into expanding the church's Sunday school program, and then left Schenectady after two short years, heading to another church in New Jersey. In December of 1903, Lunn was named Zelie's successor, the 17th pastor in the history of the church.

The man primarily responsible for Lunn coming to Schenectady was Union College professor and First Reformed elder Frank S. Hoffman. Active in First Reformed's Prospect Hill Chapel on East Liberty Street, where many working-class and immigrant families worshipped, Hoffman invited Lunn to speak at First Reformed on November 22, 1903 and he accepted the offer. Later, Lunn remembered that sermon as "one of the most radical" he had ever delivered, but regardless, within a month had received a call from the congregation and agreed to become its new pastor.

Lunn, his wife and their first child George Jr., only a year old, moved to Schenectady with great fanfare. A daughter, Mabel, would arrive later in their first year, Elizabeth two years later in 1906, Raymond in 1909 and Eleanor in 1911. Lunn's acceptance letter was printed in the Schenectady Union, and his first sermon, "Forgetting the Things Which are Behind: Reaching Forth to the Things Which are Before," was published in its entirety in the Schenectady Gazette. Everyone seemed pleased with their new minister, and the consistory voted to purchase a house on Front Street to serve as Lunn's home, even though the offer bringing him to Schenectady had stated that the position did not include a parsonage.

CHAPTER 4

Old Time Religion

Lunn's first year in Schenectady was eventful. He increased appropriations to aid poor church members. Along with his own Sunday sermons, he brought in dozens of ministers and other speakers from outside the region, including Danish-American social reformer Jacob Riis, also a New York Tribune reporter, and his presentation on "The Battle of the Slums." Lunn also started up a men's club "to encourage a more intimate acquaintance among the men of the congregation and to secure their associated services in advancing the general interest of the church." The club's initial meeting on April 14, 1904 was a huge success, attracting 164 men.

As rewarding and productive as Lunn's first year was in Schenectady, his second was extraordinary. His preaching had not only begun to fill the pews at First Reformed, it also was gaining notice around the city. In January of 1905, as Lunn began his second year at First Reformed, a religious revival took place largely in the Northeast and Midwest, as well as a few other regions of the country. For four consecutive weeks, a spiritual fervor hit Schenectady that far surpassed anything else the city had ever seen. Eighteen other protestant pastors in the city were involved, and all concurred that the man to lead the revival was Lunn. Invited to help him spur on the masses was a 27-year-old deaconess from New York City named Bertha Sanford.

Born in 1878 to wealthy parents, she attended Mt. Vernon High School and then went on to study nursing at Columbia University and Smith College in Northampton, Massachusetts, where she graduated with the class of 1900. When she was invited to Schenectady as part of International Prayer Week in December 1904 by the Rev. Fred Winslow Adams of the State Street Episcopal Methodist Church (now First United Methodist), Sanford was finishing up at Sibley Memorial Hospital in Washington, D.C., where she was a part of the national training school for deaconesses and missionaries. According to newspaper accounts, she was "pretty and possessed a beautiful singing voice," and was also quite "cordial and unaffected."

Meetings were held every day in January throughout the city at various churches and other sites, and at night the largest religious venue in town, the State Street Methodist Episcopal Church, was often filled to capacity. Lunn spoke every day and sometimes three times a day, usually sharing the pulpit with Miss Sanford and Rev. Adams. On Sunday night, January 8, when it was becoming apparent that something very special was happening in the city, the Methodist church was packed with men and women standing in the aisles as well as the choir gallery and behind the altar.

After a few introductory remarks by Rev. Adams, Sanford rose and told the audience her faith story.

"If I thought you had all come out of curiosity alone, and if I thought you had no desire to hear the message, I do not think I would feel inclined to go on with the service," she began. "Rather than tell you the story of why I became a deaconess, I would rather desire to appeal to you to receive the Saviour. It may be, though, that I can better bring my message by telling you the story. It was all a few years ago, but to me it seems an age."

Sanford told the crowd how she felt called to God at the age of 11 after attending a huge gathering much like the one to which she was now speaking. As she got older, however, she became more interested in literature, science and the theater, and felt herself drifting toward those secular endeavors before God called again near the end of her time at Smith College.

"It was just at the close of my college life that the ray of light came," she said. "Only those who have experienced the call can understand what that means. I said, 'I will go where Thou wouldst have me to go,' and it seemed that God put the seal on this, my second consecration. I had no longer any desire for my former pleasures of the theatre and dance."

Sanford, who often played the zither while singing, finished with a song, enchanting the estimated throng of 2,000 people. For many, this Sunday night offering at the Methodist church was also their first opportunity to hear Lunn. When the deaconess sat down and the minister got up to speak, the excitement was palpable. Typically, Lunn was not animated in the pulpit and certainly didn't preach fire and brimstone. According to one newspaper, Lunn's "natural manner of speaking is not emotional, appealing more to the intellect and conscience."

However, within a few moments of starting to talk this particular night, the Gazette reported he was "overcome with remorse and wept upon the pulpit." The Union-Star reported that "the full conception of fatherly love of God and his forgiveness seemed to overwhelm the speaker. For one or two minutes he seemed to be dealing alone with his God, oblivious of any audience."

Whatever Lunn was experiencing, it moved his audience the Gazette reported. "When the spasms of grief and remorse had passed and the minister buried his face on the alter and wept, the audience was weeping with him. There were handkerchiefs out all through the main auditorium and the gallery. Miss Sanford was weeping, and even strong men were drawing their hands across their eyes."

Here Lunn regrouped. "I suppose I ought to apologize for creating this scene," he said. Then, he called for those to confess their faith and "people rose and hands went up throughout the auditorium. When these came forward after the service they were of all denominations," the Gazette reported.

Throughout the month, people came from all over the region to hear Lunn and Sanford. Some drove their own automobiles from Albany and Troy, others came by horse and carriage, took the trolley or came by train from cities and towns like Fonda, Amsterdam and Saratoga. There were even reports of men walking from their farms in Glenville and Ballston Lake, 10 miles away.

While it was the International Prayer Week, initiated by the YMCA, that precipitated the revival in Schenectady, it was the

Schenectady Ministerial Association, led by Adams, that took ownership of the movement. The group wrote an open letter to the people of Schenectady which both newspapers printed. It read:

"The Ministerial Association of this city has interpreted the events of last week as God's call for service to the churches of Schenectady. We believe God has especially called out from our members as a leader the Rev. George R. Lunn, and that the coming among us of Miss Bertha Sanford of Washington, was likewise providential. A great and effectual door for aggressive evangelism is opening before us. Nineteen of our churches have united in this effort, together with the YMCA, the College YMCA and YWCA. Others of different languages and creed have assured us of their prayers and sympathy.

"Therefore, we appeal to every Christian soul in our city to make everything second to God's call for service this week; to pray daily at noon for God's blessing, without which all efforts are vain, and to work as well as pray that we may take Schenectady for Christ."

On Monday night, January 9, perhaps inspired by Lunn's words and actions from the previous day, Sanford, Rev. Adams, his wife and a small group of ministers went on a mission through Schenectady's tavern community. Hitting every establishment on State Street between Ferry and Barrett Street, Sanford, the Rev. Adams and the others pleaded with the owners and their customers to change their ways and accept Jesus. The entire excursion lasted a little more than an hour, and met with varying degrees of success. Most of the owners, bartenders and customers were cordial and listened politely, either to a short lecture from Rev. Adams or a song from the duet of Sanford and Mrs. Adams. The group repeated their efforts again on Tuesday night.

Later in the month on January 24, a Tuesday afternoon, Sanford's regular visits to the YWCA and the city's schools resulted in an impromptu outpouring of religious fervor from the children of Schenectady. At 5 p.m., that day, following Sanford's regular afternoon presentation at the Emmanuel Baptist Church on Nott Terrace, just a few feet away from the Methodist church, a most unusual scene began to take shape. As Sanford walked outside the church, a large group of children began following her singing "Onward Christian Soldiers," and before long their number, according to newspaper accounts, climbed as high as 800.

"It was a grand sight," wrote the New York Sun. "These hundreds of young people marching and countermarching, meeting thousands of men on their way home from work, and singing the songs of Jesus as they marched. Happiness was pictured on the faces of the children, and the returning men workers caught the spirit of the hour. 'Good! Good! God bless you!' was frequently heard from the men. Many of them saw their own children in the ranks of the marching host, and were gladdened by the sight. It was a genuine outburst of religious feeling."

During her month-long stay in Schenectady, Sanford met and fell in love with Welton Stanford, Jr., an usher at the First Reformed Church and a member of one of Schenectady's most prominent families. His grandfather was Charles Stanford, a member of the New York State Assembly and Senate during the Civil War and post-Civil War period, and his granduncle was Leland Stanford, founder of Stanford University and a former governor of California. Welton Jr., who was busy running the family's hardware company and raising prize roosters; black-breasted red bantams, met Miss Sanford at the First Reformed Church and soon began serving as the young lady's unofficial bodyguard. When Bertha went marching through Schenectady's saloon section on that Monday and Tuesday night in early January, Stanford was at her side the entire time. They remained in touch after Sanford left Schenectady and in April of that year the couple announced their engagement at a large party held in Sanford's honor at Locust Grove, the Stanford family's large home near the city's eastern boundary. They were married in October 1906 at the New York Avenue Methodist Episcopal Church and then returned to live in Schenectady.

While Sanford was "the most powerful yet most unassuming" aspect of Schenectady's revival according to the New York Sun, she officially left her deaconess position to marry Stanford. But her efforts at God's work never ended until her death in 1965. She became heavily involved in the Women's Home Missionary Society, and in 1911 gained more notoriety for her part in the Edith Melber murder trial. When Melber, a Schenectady woman was charged with the murder of her own child and tried in Syracuse, Mrs. Stanford traveled to the proceedings to offer comfort to the defendant, who pleaded not guilty by reason of insanity. Stanford, accompanied by her sister-in-law Mrs. Grant Stanford, told reporters in Syracuse that they were there simply to "show sympathy at a time when she [Melber] is surrounded by a throng composed either of indifferent persons or of people morbidly curious." Stanford added that she and her sister-in-law were "interested in the sufferings of this poor unfortunate, and are convinced that this woman is more to be pitied than censured. We are convinced she was not in her right mind." Melber was convicted of murder and sent to the Auburn Prison for Women with a sentence of not less than 20 years. While it was the fight for Melber's "spiritual welfare" that most concerned Bertha, she apparently also lost that battle. On March 4, 1916, Melber was found hanging in her cell, a suicide victim.

Bertha and her husband lived for the next three decades in Schenectady, Detroit and Brooklyn. When Welton Stanford died in 1947, Bertha was the nursing education director at Prospect Heights Hospital in Brooklyn. She had also been nursing supervisor at hospitals in Amsterdam and Auburn. When she retired, she returned to Schenectady and began attending services at St. John the Evangelist Church. On September 16, 1965, at the age of 87, Bertha Sanford Stanford died at the Steadwell Nursing Home on Rugby Road in Schenectady. Childless, Bertha was buried at Indian Hills Cemetery in Middletown, Conn.

Lunn, meanwhile, missed one day of preaching during Schenectady's "great crusade of aggressive evangelism" due to a cold. At the conclusion of the four weeks, he was "completely exhausted and almost collapsed" after the final meeting at the Methodist church, while Rev. Adams was also "very ill from overwork." Both men fully recovered, and soon Lunn was once again working with Sanford. The pair headlined a week's evangelical campaign at the Gospel Tent Evangel at 57th Street and Broadway in Manhattan the first week in March and again in July.

A few weeks before Lunn's second visit to Manhattan, the First Reformed celebrated its 225th anniversary, and during that same week Union College held its 109th commencement ceremony. Awarded an honorary Doctor of Divinity by the college, Lunn was well ensconced in the community just 16 months after his arrival from New York City. Schenectady's revival was one of the most fervent that cropped up around the country during that winter season of 1904-05. The work of Lunn, Sanford and the others in Schenectady gained national attention, as did revivals in Atlanta, Pittsburgh, Philadelphia, Boston, Denver and New York City.

The movement seemed to start with the awakening of Pennsylvania Welshman in December 1904, following a revival that began a few months earlier in Wales, where a reported 100,000 had been converted. Church historian Dr. Rev. Tudur Jones, writing in the 1960s, said that the Welsh revival was "the most stunning happening in the history of 20th Century Wales," but some Welsh ministers around at the time weren't so enamored with the proceedings. One, according to Jones, wrote that there was something "lamentable rather than creative about the revival in that people soon turned to politics, to the new theology and social struggles."

CHAPTER 5

Mother Jones and Other Socialists

In July of 1902, District Attorney Reese Blizzard stood up in a West Virginia courtroom, pointed at Mary Harris Jones and said, "Your honor, there sits the most dangerous woman in America."

By then, Mary Harris Jones was better known as "Mother Jones," one of the leading figures in the labor movement of that time. She was a woman who had been dealt some cruel blows. Her husband and their four children all died during the Yellow Fever Epidemic of 1867, and then four years later all her possessions, including a dressmaking business, were lost to the Great Chicago Fire of 1871.

In the final two decades of the 19th century, Jones became famous as a community organizer and strike leader, working with the Knights of Labor and then the Industrial Workers of the World (the "Wobblies") to fight for better working conditions and wages. In June, 1902, Jones travelled to West Virginia where she was jailed for organizing a miner's strike and then ignoring a court order banning any meetings by striking workers. She often fought specifically for the wives and children of striking workers, but her struggle against corporate America and the elite ruling class didn't extend to women's suffrage. Jones thought that juvenile delinquency was the result of motherly neglect, thus she didn't feel the need to be politically active. She often said, "you don't need the vote to raise hell."

Judge John J. Jackson sentenced Jones to 60 days in jail, but then suspended his order and instead gave her a lecture in the packed courthouse, suggesting that she "follow the lines and path which the Allwise Being intended her sex should pursue." Jackson also told Jones she shouldn't allow herself to be used by "outside agitators," and that there were many charities and other good works she could perform, "as experience has shown to be the true sphere of womanhood."

Jones politely declined the judge's advice. She said she would probably be arrested again, and when it happened, "I expect to receive the same punishment as the working man." She also pointed out to Jackson that they were both very old, and how she hoped when they soon met in heaven they could be friends. The courtroom erupted into laughter.

Jones was one of many colorful characters of the late 19th and early 20th centuries that helped bring national attention to workers' woes. A few months after Jones left the West Virginia courtroom, another person concerned with the plight of the poor, Daniel De Leon, was making the second of his three tries to take up residence in the governor's mansion in Albany. A newspaper editor and union organizer, De Leon ran on the Socialist Labor Party ticket and collected 15,886 votes, his highest total ever but still just fifth-best in a six-man field. Like Mother Jones, De Leon had experienced some cruel personal tragedies years earlier; the death of his young wife while delivering stillborn twins, and the loss of his one-year-old son, both in 1887.

An 1878 graduate of Columbia University, De Leon was a staunch Marxist who became a member of the SLP in 1890 and remained with that group after it splintered in 1899. While several disaffected elements of the SLP joined forces with the three-year-old Social Democratic Party of America in 1901 to form the Socialist Party of America, De Leon remained with the more radical faction. He was convinced that progressives and reformers were part of the problem. De Leon argued that society should be changed drastically, not modestly, and referred to the reform movement as a lure, or bait, designed to keep people satisfied with capitalism.

In 1905 in Chicago, the different parts of the leftist movement in America came together long enough to form the Industrial Workers of the World. Eugene Debs of the Socialist Party of America, "Big" Bill Haywood of the Western Federation of

Miners, and De Leon and his Socialist Labor Party held what Haywood dubbed the "Continental Congress of the Working Class." Haywood, however, in his desire to see the IWW gain strength, would prove too radical for Debs' taste, and subsequently more splintering would occur. While the two men remained friendly, by 1913 Haywood left the Socialist Party and Debs had cut any direct ties to the IWW, suggesting that it supported anarchy.

De Leon, meanwhile, had problems with Haywood even earlier. In 1908, he argued that political action – largely through his Socialist Labor Party – was the best way for the IWW to fight its battles. Haywood and others, however, were convinced that direct action in the form of strikes and boycotts would better serve the working class. Haywood won the argument. De Leon and his supporters left the IWW and formed a rival group that also called itself the IWW . It was renamed the Workers International Industrial Union in 1915, a year after De Leon's death. However, without his leadership, the group eventually collapsed in 1925, and while the Socialist Labor Party continued on, it never garnered the mainstream attention achieved by Debs and his brand of socialism. De Leon remained a revered figure for most Socialists throughout the first half of the 20th century, but politically he never was a great vote-getter. Even in 1902, when De Leon got nearly 16,000 votes in the race for governor of New York and finished fifth, Benjamin Hanford, the standard bearer for the less radical Social Democratic ticket, was clearly the more popular candidate, finishing third with 23,400 votes.

Hanford wasn't the intellectual that De Leon was, but he was more likable. A Cleveland native, he had a newspaper background like De Leon, but had very little education and was a plain workingman, having joined the Chicago Typographical Union after learning the printing trade. For 30 years he went through life with little passion before converting to socialism.

"I was in the gutter," Hanford wrote, "when socialism came and gave me something to live for. Socialism is life. Next to having socialism, the greatest thing in the world is to work for socialism."

A fine orator, Hanford caught the eye of Eugene Debs in 1904 and was asked by the Socialists' national political leader to be his vice-presidential candidate on the Socialist ticket that year and again in 1908. Along with his 1902 gubernatorial run, Hanford ran two other times for governor and once for mayor of New York, all unsuccessfully. Hanford died in 1910 and is reputed to have scribbled while on his death bed, "I would that my every heart's beat should have been for the working class, and through them for all humanity."

As colorful and impressive figures as Jones, Haywood, De Leon and Hanford were, they and all other Socialists at the time lived in the immense shadow of Debs. Born in Terre Haute, Indiana, Nov. 5, 1855, Debs dropped out of school at the age of 14 and began working as a painter and then a boilerman for the railroads. In 1874, after attending business school at night, Debs returned to Terre Haute and began working as a grocery clerk. In 1875 he became a founding member and recording secretary of the Brotherhood of Locomotive Firemen, and by 1880 was the editor of the group's magazine and Grand Secretary. All this activity spurred his entry into politics, and in 1884 he was voted into the Indiana State Assembly as a Democrat for one term.

Ten years later, however, when the American Railway Union was on strike against the Pullman Palace Car Company, the sight of American troops firing on their own citizens had a profound effect on Debs. One of the leaders of the strike, Debs was still a Democrat when he entered federal prison in Woodstock, Illinois, having been arrested for failing to obey an injunction against the strike and for conspiracy to stop delivery of the U.S. mail. Clarence Darrow, one of the top lawyers of the day and later the defense attorney in the Scopes Monkey Trial in Dayton, Tennessee, couldn't clear Debs. However, five months later when he left jail in 1895, Debs had converted to socialism due to the influence of Martin J. Elliott, director of the American Railway Union, who had also been imprisoned for leading the strike in St. Louis.

With its leaders jailed, the strike fizzled, but not before 12 workers had been shot and killed by federal troops. The work stoppage proved costly to the railroads, but with the support of then-president Grover Cleveland, the federal government clearly indicated its willingness to intervene on the side of big corporations over the interests of the workforce. Along with Debs and Elliott, a total of 71 workers were arrested because of the strike, and the experience left Debs forever suspicious of the wealthy ruling class, and firmly embedded his sympathies with the poor working men and women of America. In 1900, Debs launched his first presidential campaign and Elliott tried for a seat in the U.S. House of Representatives. Both lost, although Elliott would later be elected as a Socialist to the Montana State Legislature.

Through the first two decades of the 20th century, Debs would continue to enthrall audiences with his speaking ability and the overall goodness he seemed to exude. New York newspaperman John Swinton heard both Abraham Lincoln and Debs captivate crowds at Cooper Union in New York City, and felt like there was little separating the two men.

"I recall the appearance, the manner, the voice and the speech of Lincoln as Debs stood before me 34 years afterwards," wrote Swinton. "It seemed to me that both men were imbued with the same spirit. Both seemed to me as men of judgment, reason, earnestness and power. Both seemed to me as men of free, high, genuine and generous manhood. I took to Lincoln in my early life as I took to Debs a third of a century later."

In 1917 Debs was jailed by the Wilson administration based on the Espionage Act and was sentenced to a 10-year prison term. Wilson refused to pardon Debs, calling him a traitor because he encouraged young men to resist the draft during World War I. But on Dec. 21, 1921, Warren G. Harding commuted Deb's sentence to time served and even greeted him at the White House the day after he left an Atlanta penitentiary. Later that week a crowd estimated at 50,000 met Debs at the train station when he arrived back home in Terre Haute. He died in 1926, a few weeks shy of his 71st birthday.

CHAPTER 6

Muckrakers and Anarchists

The struggle of the poor working class at the turn of the 20th century did not go unnoticed. New legislation initiated by President Teddy Roosevelt, including the Pure Food and Drug Act and the Meat Inspection Act in 1906, were a direct result of investigative journalism that brought to light corruption and other forms of social injustice perpetrated on the poor by the wealthy. Roosevelt initially applauded this type of ground-breaking journalistic endeavor, and when the work of newspaper writers like Julius Chambers, Nellie Bly, Lincoln Steffens and Ida Tarbell was added to the reaction from novels like Theodore Dreiser's "Sister Carrie" (1900) and Upton Sinclair's "The Jungle" (1906), the Progressive Era (1890-1920) was in full bloom. In 1906, however, another writer, David Graham Phillips, published an article in "Cosmopolitan" describing corruption in the U.S. Senate. Many of its members, some of them allies of Roosevelt, were singled out by Phillips, and the president was not happy. In a speech before the U.S. House of Representatives, Roosevelt added a new entry to the American lexicon when he compared these writers to the muck-raker in John Bunyan's "Pilgrim's Progress." Roosevelt said, "the man who could look no way but downward with the muck-rake in his hands; who would neither look up nor regard the crown he was offered, but continued to rake to himself the filth on the floor."

Suddenly, investigative journalists were called muckrakers, clearly not a term of endearment at the time. Steffens and other progressive journalists felt they had helped elect Roosevelt in 1904 – Roosevelt defeated Democratic candidate Alton B. Parker of New York, 56.4-37.6 percent – and they were upset at what seemed like Roosevelt's repudiation of their work. Then, life changed when the U.S. entered World War I in 1917, and some of the journalists on the extreme left that had been attracted to Communism headed across the Atlantic Ocean and Europe to cover the Russian Revolution. Steffens was one of those writers and declared that he had "seen the future, and it works." Like many others, however, after seeing the Russian version of communism close up, he became disenchanted with the idea and returned to the U.S., still claiming, however, that the economic system of capitalism was the reason for social corruption.

The "Muckraker Era" is therefore closely aligned with the Progressive Era. It was Julius Chambers' New York Tribune piece about the Bloomingdale Asylum in 1872 that is often cited as the first example of muckracking, but it would take some time for the public response to build and subsequently create serious political action. Forty years after Chambers told the sad tale of the mentally handicapped, Woodrow Wilson and Roosevelt were both claiming the Progressive label during the 1912 presidential election. They wound up finishing one-two respectively in the voting ahead of the conservative incumbent William Howard Taft and the liberal Debs. However, with World War I just a few years away, both the Progressive Era and the Muckraker Era would draw to a close as the U.S. had what was perceived by most a much bigger threat in Germany than in the capitalistic endeavors of billionaires like J.P. Morgan and John D. Rockefeller.

In November 1906, Charles Evans Hughes, a man moderate enough to be referred to as both progressive and conservative, won the governorship of New York by beating the liberal Democratic candidate and newspaper magnate William Randolph Hearst. Hughes, a Glens Falls native, was the only Republican that year to win statewide office.

As an editorial in the Schenectady Gazette pointed out, something was up with the electorate of New York State.

"It was an election in which party lines were broken to an unusual degree. Men asserted their independence of leaders and bosses, and cast their ballots as they deemed best. Former affiliations and life-long voting habits counted for little."

Workingmen – women had yet to get the vote in New York State – were beginning to feel as if they might have some say in their future. Yet, efforts to improve their quality of life were usually met with strong resistance. In December 1906, Hans Schwartz and Louis Basky, two draftsmen at the General Electric Company in Schenectady, were both dismissed from their jobs for their union organizing efforts. At 2 p.m., on a Monday afternoon, Dec. 10, in what was the first "sit-in" strike in American history, about 3,000 IWW workers at GE in sympathy with Schwartz and Basky, turned off their machines and just sat, refusing to do any work. The strike was not supported by the American Federation of Labor, which didn't recognize the IWW and ordered its union members and all their affiliates to continue working.

"We do not recognize the Industrial Workers of the World as a bonafide labor organization, or its members as union members," said the AF of L in a written press release. "As to any individual organization affiliated with the AF of L going out in a sympathetic strike, such action would result in forfeiture of its charter.... We are extremely dis-interested in the present dispute."

Just 10 days after initiating the strike, the IWW told its GE workers to go back to work. The strike was called off.

On Dec. 16, during the middle of the work stoppage, Lunn, still a minister at the First Reformed and a registered Republican, spoke in front of a large audience, many of them striking workers, at the Lyceum Academy. Lunn didn't mention the GE-IWW situation in Schenectady, but he did argue for the concept of "industrial democracy." And, while the headline in the Schenectady Gazette the next day roared, "Socialism Not the Cure Says Lunn," it is clear from his words that he was most sympathetic toward the striking workers.

"Practically, therefore, men are agreed that democracy is eternally right for the government, church and for the public school," said Lunn. "Shall the principle of democracy be further applied to and control industry?"

While calling GE general manager George E. Emmons "honest, upright and well-meaning," he reminded those in attendance of the words of Andrew Carnegie a week earlier in New York City at a Civic Federation meeting: "Wealth is made by community."

"When these men die," said Lunn, referring to Carnegie and other millionaires from that era, "the community fails in its duty, and our legislators fail in their duty, if they do not exact a tremendous share, a progressive share. It is not the millionaire who makes the wealth. Wealth, gentlemen, is based upon the community.

"If the people as a whole produce the wealth of a nation, why was it that in 1899 one percent of the families of the U.S. owned more of the general wealth than did the other 99 percent?" asked Lunn, who was repeatedly interrupted by applause from the audience. "As they objected to the concentration of political power in an oligarchy, so they will object to the concentration of industrial power in a plutocracy," summed up Lunn. "As they have received that the people will control their political, their educational and ecclesiastical institutions, so they are coming to the resolve that the people shall control their industrial organizations."

Aside from the nice words about Emmons, it was the kind of rhetoric that someone like Lucy Parsons or Emma Goldman would have cheered. It was Parsons, the wife of Albert Parsons, one of the four men hanged for their involvement in the Chicago Haymarket Riots in 1886, who first proposed a "sit-down" strike at the inaugural IWW meeting in 1905.

"My conception of the strike of the future is not to strike and go out and starve but to strike and remain in and take possession of the necessary property of production," said Parsons, and just over a year later that's exactly what the Wobblies did in Schenectady - at least to a degree. The GE workers remained at their machines not working for about 65 hours, receiving food from family and friends before they finally left the premises and headed home.

Parsons' story, like those of Mother Jones and other radical socialists, is compelling. She was born in Texas in 1853, perhaps as a slave since she was a mix of African, Mexican and Native-American ethnicity. Her husband, who fought for the Confederacy during the Civil War at the age of 13, eventually found himself supporting the rights of Blacks as well as all working men as a socialist and anarchist newspaper editor. On May 4, 1886, Albert Parsons spoke to the striking railroad workers at a peaceful rally in Chicago's Haymarket Square. When rain started falling later in the day, Parsons, Lucy and their two children headed to nearby Zeph's Hall for some food and drink. At 10 p.m,. that night, as the rally was already breaking up, policemen told the people to disperse. Someone threw a bomb killing an officer, and the cops responded by shooting into the crowd and killing seven people. Parsons, who had peacefully led 80,000 people down Michigan Avenue just four days earlier on May 1 in support of the eight-hour workday – the first May Day Parade – wasn't initially arrested. Eventually, however, he turned himself into authorities as a show of solidarity with the other seven anarchists that had been jailed after the incident. They were all convicted of murder, and on Nov. 10, 1887, Parsons was one of four men executed by hanging.

His wife, an excellent public speaker, continued to fight for working men and women throughout her life, and died in 1942 at the age of 89. In 2004, a small park in the northwest section of Chicago was named Lucy Parsons Park in her honor.

Parsons' affection for socialism somewhat diluted her significance among more staunch anarchists like Goldman, who was a more radical member of that group and later was involved in the 1892 assassination attempt against Henry Clay Frick, chairman of the Carnegie Steel Company. Goldman's long-time lover and fellow anarchist Alexander Berkman shot Frick twice and also stabbed him but failed to inflict any mortal damage. Frick, who was targeted by Berkman because of the Homestead Strike and his role in hiring Pinkertons who shot and killed nine workers, was back at work in a week. Berkman was arrested and sent to jail where he served 14 years of a 22-year sentence. Goldman never showed remorse for the attempt on Frick's life, although she reputedly told a friend much later that "at the age of 23, one does not reason."

In 1901, when anarchist Leon Czolgosz shot and killed President William McKinley in Buffalo, Goldman was arrested and jailed for two weeks for "planning the assassination." In truth, although Czolgosz had tried to associate himself with Goldman and had attempted to enter her inner circle, she and her group distanced themselves from him, thinking he was an undercover policeman. After she was released from jail, Goldman offered to nurse McKinley back to health since he was "merely a human being." But she never condemned Czolgosz's act and was thus vilified in the press, which referred to her as the "high priestess of anarchy."

In January of 1908, Goldman, a little older and wiser, showed up in Schenectady and spoke on the subject of 'Syndicalism," a system that allowed for labor unions to be in charge of all means of production and distribution. Born in 1869 in present-day Lithuania and what was then part of the Russian empire, Goldman emigrated to New York City in 1885 and initially became attracted to anarchism due to the Haymarket Riot a year later. Along with Berkman, she became a popular proponent of anarchism through her speeches and writings, but by 1908, well after the Frick and McKinley shootings, her rhetoric had grown less volatile. She toured New York cities that month, speaking on January 12 at Utica on "What Anarchism Really Stands For," on January 13 and 14 in Albany on "Trade Unionism" and "The Woman in the Future," and on January 15 in Gloversville on "Trade Unionism" again.

On January 16, Goldman came to Schenectady. Mayor Horace Van Voast said that Goldman would be allowed to speak, but that city officials would be in attendance and if she did say something "objectionable," or if there was any "firebug talk," the police would immediately shut down her presentation.

According to the Schenectady Gazette's report the next day, Goldman's talk was "mild and tame." The article focused on Goldman's appearance more than what she said, referring to her as a "chunky little woman with spectacles and a loud voice," and added that she had a "well-fed appearance and a general rotund look that was beyond the chubby stage. In fact, she came far from being impressive."

The newspaper also played down the response to Goldman's talk, held at the Electrical Workers' Union Hall on State Street, writing that most of the men left "disappointed." However, Goldman's own recollection rated the visit a highlight of her tour, later writing in "Mother Earth" that "Schenectady gave the largest audience and a very enthusiastic one at that."

Julius Seltzer, a Jewish anarchist who lived in Schenectady from 1907-11, was one of the individuals responsible for bringing Goldman to the city, and in an oral interview in 1972 remembered that Goldman was well received by the GE and ALCO workers who attended her talk. "It was an enormous success, with an overflow crowd." Seltzer also remarked that Goldman was "affectionate, always hugging me and squeezing me…. She was a homely woman, but once she mounted the rostrum she became a different woman, beaming with fire, beautiful in her Spanish shawl."

Goldman was deported to Russia in 1917, spoke out against the Bolshevik Revolution once the Soviet regime had become too violent, and lived out much of her life in Toronto, dying in 1940 at the age of 70.

She and Parsons were never friendly, and remained at odds their entire lives over the details of their struggle against capitalism, including how class politics and gender and sexual issues related to the cause. Like Mother Jones, both Parsons and Goldman opted out of the first wave of feminism, showing little inclination to immerse themselves into the women's suffrage movement.

CHAPTER 7

Leaving First Reformed

Three months before the sit-down strike at GE, Lunn had been elected president of the Schenectady Classis for the Reformed Church of America. There were 14 churches in all, including two Reformed churches in downtown Schenectady, and two others within the city limits in Mont Pleasant and Bellevue. There were also two Reformed churches in Scotia, Rotterdam and Glenville, as well as single congregations in Altamont, Princetown, Vischer's Ferry , Guilderland and Lisha Kill.

While Lunn's sermons and preaching style always commanded the congregation's attention, after a while some critics emerged saying he demonstrated a "lack of balance." Also, by 1907 his preaching had become a bit more pointed and precise, addressing such topics as "The Anomaly of Child Labor in a Christian Land," and "The Relation of Jesus to Politics." In 1908 he started holding special Thursday night classes on "Social Christianity," and in the fall of that year began citing specific instances of governmental corruption in the city.

He was unquestionably the most popular and charismatic minister in the city. On February 8, 1908, when William Jennings Bryan, the great Populist and three-time Democratic candidate for president, got off a train in Schenectady he immediately went to a private reception at Lunn's home on Union Street. Later that day, when the "Great Commoner," spoke in front of a standing room only audience at the Methodist Church downtown, it was Lunn who introduced him. As Lunn's star continued to rise, so too did the number of his detractors and their ferocity. On October 8, 1908, Lunn called a special meeting of the consistory to address some of the issues and criticisms that had been voiced by a small group of church members regarding his social ministry. What was discussed and Lunn's response to it was "laid on the table" according to the church history of the First Reformed produced by Kathryn Sharp Pontius, Gerald F. DeJong and Rev Dr. J. Dean Dykstra, and wasn't revisited until a year later in November 1909. Before then, however, Lunn wrote various letters detailing his problems with the consistory.

"When I tell you that I am in the most aristocratic and wealthiest church of this city of 80,000, you will know that I am having a pretty hard battle, standing as I do openly for the new spiritual movement and for socialism," wrote Lunn in a letter to a Mr. Campbell, dated February 27, 1909.

On April 12, 1909, he wrote to Rev. Dr. David Gregg, his mentor during his time at Lafayette Avenue Presbyterian Church in Brooklyn, "No one deprecates more than I do the bringing into the pulpit of any political or economic program. I do believe, however, that there are special times when the wrongs of the present industrial order are suitable subjects for the pulpit."

And, on May 25 of that year, Lunn wrote to his father, "Last night for the first time, someone said that I had been preaching Socialism since last fall. Another member said, 'No, I don't think he has brought Socialism into the pulpit at all.' Another man wisely remarked that if Socialism and Christianity were so near together that it was a debate as to which was which there must be something in common after all, to which I replied, 'I believe Socialism was simply Christianity applied.'"

Lunn also told his father that the consistory conceded that "the great mass of the congregation were with me, but that the number against was so formidable that they believed I ought to resign." Five of the eight members of consistory felt Lunn should resign according to his letter, while "the other three were just as violently in my behalf."

On Oct. 24, 1909, Lunn announced during his Sunday sermon that he would be leaving, effective January 1, 1910, and on Nov. 1, 1909, Lunn handed the consistory a written statement confirming what he had said earlier. He did not present his resignation to the congregation, in deference to the consistory's belief that it would create a great rift in the church, and instead offered it to the consistory so that they would take whatever action they thought would be best for the church.

"I believe that the wrongs of the present industrial order are suitable subjects for the Christian pulpit; the great question of poverty and its causes; the question of wealth and its responsibilities; civic conditions; the cruelties of child labor, are not only subjects for the Christian pulpit, but to discuss them constitutes an obligation resting upon the Christian minister," Lunn wrote. "Because of this I have received the opposition of a strong minority of this church so diametrically opposed to that of your pastor that a continuance of our present relations is impossible unless a long continued struggle is entered into."

It was a fight Lunn could have won. When the consistory did poll the adult members of the congregation, only 104 voted to accept Lunn's resignation; 281 were not in favor, showing their support of Lunn, while 26 abstained. But on November 22, the consistory voted, 7-1, to accept the resignation, Maxwell Day being the lone voice on behalf of Lunn.

A native of Honeoye in western New York, Day had been an engineer for the Thomson-Houston Electrical Company in Lynn, Mass. When that firm merged with Edison's company to form GE in 1894, Day came to Schenectady and joined the First Reformed Church. By 1909 he was a leading researcher with GE and a deacon and Sunday School superintendent with the First Reformed. While consistory was made up of the upper middle class, only Day and Ernest J. Berggren (an accountant) had any connection to GE, often the target of Lunn sermons. The other members of consistory were John C. Van Voast (an attorney), Dr. Garrett V. Johnson (a physician), Frank J. Walton (a Schenectady Clothing Company employee), Matthew Winne (the Assistant Postmaster), James H. Stoller (a Union College professor) and Dr. A.R. Brubacher (the superintendent of the Schenectady school district.). But Day's support of Lunn evidently didn't hurt his career at GE. He continued to work there successfully until 1930, earning 13 patents while also becoming head of the company's marine department.

The consistory gave Lunn a vacation with full pay from January 1 through May 10, 1910, and in March of that year sent out a call to Rev. Clayton J. Potter of Simsbury, Conn. A Schenectady County native who grew up on a farm in Glenville, Potter was the great-grandnephew of Dirk Romeyn, a senior pastor at First Reformed just following the American Revolution. Potter remained at First Reformed for 27 years, and while competent and popular, he didn't fill the pews like Lunn. According to church records, the number of members in full communion in 1909 were 559. By 1914 that number had dropped to 352, and throughout much of the next three decades the church endured great financial struggles.

Lunn, meanwhile, gave his last sermon at First Reformed on January 2, 1910. He spoke at both morning services that day and also addressed the People's Forum at First Reformed in the afternoon. On the next day, Monday, January 3, Lunn spoke to the Schenectady Ministerial Association of Schenectady. While he was an unemployed husband and father of five, he certainly wasn't without prospects or the opportunity to continue his verbal assault on corporate greed and political corruption. He had travelled to Buffalo in December for a speaking engagement, and on January 10, 1910, his first Sunday in the unemployed ranks, he lectured at Albany's First Congregational Church on the subject, "The Socialistic Possibilities of the Church." Also, while Lunn was pondering his future during the first half of that month, others were doing the legwork to make sure he would continue to preach in Schenectady. A petition urging Lunn to create his own church had been circulating throughout the city, and by the third week in January, 1,500 signatures had been collected. All of the signers had been male, the majority of them "working wagemen" according to Lunn.

"If I stay in Schenectady it will be because I want to do the work for which I feel I have a call," Lunn told the Gazette on January 25. "If I were going after the money I could accept a place which offers great inducements in the line of salary. I am not considering that phase of the proposition yet."

Lunn stayed in Schenectady. On January 27, the Gazette informed its readers that Lunn's new church would conduct its first service on Sunday evening, February 6, at the Mohawk Theatre. Along with the 1,500 signatures, Lunn disclosed that he had several wealthy backers who would eventually see to it that the congregation would have its own new building.

On that Sunday evening of February 6, Lunn spoke before 1,200 people, which wasn't quite a full house at the Mohawk Theatre on South College Street, a stone's throw from the Erie Canal. He talked about the "spontaneous movement" to create the church and how "the degree of enthusiasm was "most gratifying." Lunn's sermon was titled, "The Church and the Masses," but he also talked about the future of his congregation.

"I have suggested the plan of arranging this series of Sunday evening services for a period of two months and test the solid strength of that support necessary to carry on so important an endeavor," said Lunn. "If the number now interested remain faithful to the new movement, we shall then organize a People's Church, whose purpose shall be as broad as human life. As deep as human need."

On February 5, the day before his new church opened, Lunn was back in Buffalo speaking on "The Basis of the New Social Order," and his drumbeat never stopped. Along with his church sermons and various speaking engagements around the Northeast, Lunn also started up a weekly newspaper, "The Citizen," which hit the streets of Schenectady for the first time on May 20 and offered him another medium to attract people to the cause. The paper had plenty of commercial support, getting large ads from city businesses such as the Carl Company, the Wallace Company and the H.S. Barney Company, and was also welcomed by Utica's Daily Observer, a newspaper dating back to 1848. "In Hoc Signo Vinces," wrote the Observer, the Latin rendering of an ancient Greek phrase that means "in this sign you will conquer." The Observer also wrote about The Citizen, "may it always have a cheering word of welcome for the laboring man."

In August, Lunn was invited to Pittsfield, Massachusetts, and delivered an address entitled, "How Cities can be Governed," an even stronger indication of his socialist sympathies. While he had been a registered Republican, and many from that party wanted him to run for mayor on their ticket, Lunn refrained from getting too cozy with any political group. Then, on December 9, 1910, the Gazette headline informed its readers what most of them had long expected: Lunn had become an official member of the local Socialist Party.

"I was an enrolled Republican last year, but I have never been a hide-bound member of any party," Lunn told the newspaper. "You know that my leanings have been socialistic, because I think the principles of the Socialist Party the most sound. I always have been affiliated with the Republicans, but more as an independent than anything else, although I have supported [William Jennings] Bryan. In the past my republicanism can be explained by the fact that I had to affiliate with some party, and so far as certain of its tenets went, the Republican Party made the large appeal to me."

Lunn sounded convinced that his affiliation with the Socialist Party would be the most important and long-lasting of his life.

"The emblem of the uplifted torch is mine hereafter," he said. "I do not think either of the two great parties hold out promises of solution of the problems that confront us. I believe the Socialist Party does. I did not join the party in the hope of immediate political success, victory at the polls or any of that sort of thing, although it will come in time. Socialism is growing."

Charles Noonan, the local Socialist party leader, immediately offered Lunn up as the group's next candidate for mayor. John C. Bellingham, the party's candidate for mayor in 1909, collected just 926 votes of the more than 13,000 cast in that election. Democrat Dr. Charles Duryee, who had been mayor back in 1898, won the 1909 contest by a slim margin (6,362 to 6,052) over Republican Everett Smith, a banker and attorney whose brother, Gerardus Smith, was a Democrat and owner of the city's morning newspaper, the Schenectady Gazette.

Although Bellingham evidently wasn't a very successful vote-getter in 1909, he became a very powerful leader of the General Electric union movement and the Socialist Party. A "sharp-tongued" Scottish immigrant, Bellingham was an electrician at GE who became president of the Schenectady Electrical Workers District Council and one of the organizers of the Schenectady Metal Trades Council. In 1916 an investigator hired by GE informed the company that Belllingham was the "most radical and perhaps the most dangerous man in the Schenectady plant." By 1916, through Bellingham's efforts, the union movement that had previously been limited to Schenectady began spreading to GE's other plants in Lynn and Pittsfield, Massachusetts, Erie, Pennsylvania, and Fort Wayne, Indiana.

In 1916, as President Wilson was contemplating how best to keep the U.S. out of World War I, Socialists and other members of the anti-war community formed a group called the American Union against Militarism, and it was Belligham who created the Schenectady chapter. After the U.S. declared war on Germany in April 1917, many in Bellingham's camp suggested that the "social struggles" of the day should be suspended during time of war. Bellingham called that kind of thinking "ridiculous advice," and added that it was not the workers who created the class struggle, and that it was "stupid in the extreme for us to try and stop this struggle of workers for their rights." In 1919, Bellingham, testifying on behalf of the Electrical Manufacturing Industry Labor Board, proudly told the National War Labor Board to "keep your eye on what Schenectady and the allied plants are doing," for "what Schenectady thinks today the U.S. does tomorrow, so far as organized labor is concerned."

Belllingham ran for political office again in 1920 but lost his bid for a seat in the state assembly. In May of that year he was also a delegate from New York to the Socialist National Convention held at the Finnish Socialist Hall in New York City.

Noonan, meanwhile, would be one of the Socialist alderman swept into power with Lunn in 1911. He remained a leader in the local party for years, running for various offices from Lt.

Governor to secretary of State. He lost 10 elections in all, continuing his fight for socialism well into the 1930s.

Despite Noonan's hearty endorsement of Lunn in the final month of 1910, it would be quite some time before the pastor actually announced his intention of running for political office. He spent much of 1911 continuing his role as an outspoken minister, newspaper editor and lecturer, continuing to voice his disapproval of the wealthy capitalists that were running America and filling their pockets with money, while the common man struggled.

Much of Lunn's tirade against political corruption fell on deaf ears. To many citizens, it was part of the cultural package and probably always would be.

Lincoln Steffens, during his days with McClure's Magazine, wrote an article in 1902 called "The Shame of the Cities," in which he hoped to outrage Americans by showing them the numerous examples of political corruption in municipalities across the country. Included in that article and other writings by Steffens were some rather pointed shots at Tammany Hall, a political organization run by Democrats that dominated New York City for more than 75 years. But George Washington Plunkitt, a ward boss, alderman and state senator who ruled the old 15th district in New York City for more than 25 years, took on Steffens' allegations head-on in very frank terms.

"Steffens means well, but like all reformers, he don't know how to make distinctions," Plunkitt told New York Evening Post Reporter William L. Riordan. "He can't see no difference between honest graft and dishonest graft and, consequent, he gets things all mixed up. There's the biggest kind of a difference between political looters and politicians who make a fortune out of politics by keeping their eyes open.... I seen my opportunities and I took 'em."

Things, however, were beginning to change, at least to some small degree. Plunkitt, who argued against civil service reform his whole life, lost his 1904 race for state assembly and never again won elected office. Younger Democrats like Al Smith were forcing Tammany Hall to improve its reputation and the way it conducted business. By Plunkitt's death in 1924 the organization hailed itself as a proponent of reform.

Steffens, meanwhile, in sharp contrast with Plunkitt, came from a wealthy family, covered the Mexican Revolution in 1910 and became a staunch proponent of communism. But, following his "I have seen the future and it works" line in 1919 while covering the Russian Revolution, his enthusiasm for communism waned. By the time he wrote his memoirs in 1931 he was markedly dissatisfied with the Russian example.

Urged on by the muckrakers, Governor Hughes began a series of investigations into municipal corruption, and during his time as governor (1907-1910) many reforms were enacted, including the Lessland Act, giving the governor the power to fire corrupt officials. Supported by Theodore Roosevelt and appointed to the Supreme Court by his successor William Howard Taft, Evans ran for the presidency himself in 1916 and lost narrowly to Woodrow Wilson.

The new governor taking office in January 1911 was John Alden Dix, like Hughes, a Glens Falls native but a Democrat. Dix served two relatively quiet years, earning credit for the formation of the State Conservation Commission, approving legislation authorizing direct primary elections and getting legislation passed limiting the number of working hours for women and children following the deadly Triangle Shirtwaist Factory fire in March 1911.

While Lunn supported all three of those innovations, Dix's record wasn't nearly progressive or reform-minded enough for Lunn, whose popularity as a speaker would reach grand new heights in 1911. Along with his church sermons (the People's Church had merged with another local parish to form the United People's Church), his newspaper editorials and his regular speaking engagements, Lunn participated in a series of debates with Albany attorney Jay W. Forrest on the issue of "Socialism vs. Progressivism." In February 1911, Forrest had been invited to speak in Lunn's absence at the Mohawk Theatre and delighted a large audience with his lecture entitled, "Our Revolutionary Forefathers." In Lunn 's newspaper that Friday, Forrest was described as "an exceptionally good speaker, and his many telling points were loudly applauded." Forrest, who made a lot of money in law and real estate, was a national chairman of the Populist Party and had been prominent in that group since the 1890s.

In his speech that day subbing for Lunn, Forrest compared corporations in the U.S. to England during the Colonial Era, suggesting that the mother country "compelled the colonies to send their products to England, and also compelled them to buy the return cargoes. A sarcastic member of the House of Commons proposed that the colonies should be compelled to send their horses to England to be shod... The system works about the same today, the difference being that our corporations take the place of England."

Forrest also said, "Show me a Rockefeller fortune and I will show you, as its logical inevitable offset, a million men who have never a surplus dollar to lay by," and "the rights of the individual person are forgotten in the clamor for the rights of the corporation person." They were words that could have been spoken by Lunn, but the distinction between Forrest and Lunn is that the latter took it further. Forrest wanted to tweak or repair capitalism. Lunn wanted to replace it with socialism.

On March 24, a Friday night, about 1,700 people squeezed into the Van Curler Theatre, the largest venue in Schenectady, to listen to Lunn and Forrest debate. Admisson was 25 cents and according to newspaper accounts, more than 500 people were turned away. The format called for each man to speak for 30 minutes and then offer a 20-minute rebuttal followed by another 10-minute summary. For the most part it was a thoughtful and polite conversation, Lunn explaining that socialists "don't want one percent to decide for the other ninety-nine percent," while Forrest countered with the notion that men had the ability to change things each election cycle, but instead "went to the polls where they voted like sheep."

On April 7, 1911, in the Odd Fellows Hall in downtown Albany, the two combatants once again argued their case in front of a packed house, their main goal to explain all the nuanced differences between socialism and radical progressivism and how their particular philosophy was the best answer for what ailed America. Forrest argued that socialism was communism, while Lunn felt there were distinct differences between the two. On May 4, Lunn and Forrest visited Darling Theatre in Gloversville to continue the series, and on May 11 went back to Fulton County, speaking at The Grand in neighboring John-stown. The two Democratic mayors of each city, Wesley Borst for Gloversville and Abram Harrison for Johnstown, served as moderators and both occasions drew large audiences. Both of those communities had large socialist organizations, and in each Friday edition of The Citizen, a couple of columns were reserved for Johnstown-Gloversville news.

The winner of each debate depended upon one's personal view or the political bent of the newspaper you were reading. All accounts gave glowing reviews of the speakers' abilities to argue their point, reporters referring to Forrest as "Bryanesque," while Lunn's oratorical skills had been finely tuned after more than a decade of speaking from the pulpit. While Lunn's newspaper suggested that its man had won the debate, it did say that "Popu-lism and reform had in Mr. Forrest a most able defender. There is no orator on the public platform today better able to cope with socialism than Mr. Forrest."

Plans were made for a fifth debate during the summer, but it never came off, The Citizen reporting that Forrest's camp was never that enthusiastic about another meeting and failed to respond to terms presented by Lunn's backers. Referred to as Albany's "Captain of the Common Good," Forrest had earlier been involved in the liberal wing of the Democratic party before aligning himself more closely with the movements of populism and progressivism. In 1902, when disaffected Democrats tried forming their own Liberal Democratic Party of New York State, Forrest had even been mentioned as a possible candidate for governor. He wrote "Tammany's Treason," a staunch defense of William Sulzer, the first New York governor to be removed from office in 1913. In 1920 he found another home as the Grand Master of the Sons and Daughters of Washington, an organi-zation which felt it was necessary to combat any influence the Catholic church might have on American politics. Despite his liberal and progressive instincts, Forrest became a staunch anti-

Catholic and less and less relevant in New York politics. In 1920, he was quoted by the New York Times, "If a man tells you he's a Catholic, you may rest assured that he is a bad American," and at a speech in New York City that same year, Forrest told an enthusiastic crowd of like-minded people, "we will make sure that the next president is either a mason or a protestant."

Lunn, meanwhile, despite Forrest's lack of appetite for a fifth debate, wasn't short on speaking opportunities in 1911. In June he welcomed Debs to Schenectady and marked Milwaukee Congressman Victor Berger's speech in the U.S. Congress that same month, the first ever delivered by a Socialist. In the first week of July, Lunn spoke in front of a large crowd at Crescent Park (now Veterans Park) in support of striking laborers in the construction business, and on July 15, he shared the stage with New York Call editor Joseph Wanhope at the first-ever picnic of the local Socialist Party at Brandywine Park. Lunn reported on his recent visit to Milwaukee where he was received by Socialist mayor Emil Seidel, and Wanhope spoke about socialism in New York City.

As for The Citizen, what had begun as Lunn's one-man operation was, by the time it celebrated its first year of operations, the public voice of the local Socialist Party. In May 1911 it was incorporated with Lunn as president, Noonan as vice-president, Hawley Van Vechten as treasurer, Rueben L. Knapp as secretary and Ben S. Henry as business manager. All were Socialists, and Lunn, Noonan and Van Vechten did much of the reporting and writing in the newspaper.

CHAPTER 9

Winning the Mayor's Office

All that summer Lunn hammered away at the corrupt municipal administration in Schenectady, his attacks including pointed
tirades at Union Paving Company president Charles Beckwith.
Lunn wrote that Beckwith should be known as the "exalted ruler
of Schenectady" because he had every city administration and
particularly the current Democratic leaders "in his back pocket."
As strongly as Lunn felt about the corruption he thought was
rampant throughout Schenectady politics, he often found himself in agreement with the ideas of Mayor Charles Duryee. When
Duryee prohibited professional boxing in Schenectady, Lunn
was in full agreement and wrote about it in The Citizen. When
Duryee argued for and received more physicians to help the city
deal with its poor and ailing population, The Citizen proclaimed
that "Mayor Duryee Has Won a Most Brilliant Victory."

As the election of 1911 loomed, the Democrats had four men
interested in running for mayor, but that number was reduced
to three when the incumbent announced on September 26 that
he would not seek another term. Duryee was the son of the Rev.
Isaac Groot Duryee, the man responsible for the creation of the
first Black church in Schenectady and pastor of Schenectady's
Second Reformed Church.

An 1838 Union College graduate, Duryee was a popular
pastor and Civil War chaplain in the 81st New York Infantry. He
never fully recovered after becoming sick with a fever in 1864,
and died in 1866 at the age of 55, leaving behind a wife and eight
children. His son Charles, the seventh child, was a very popular
physician and somewhat of a reluctant politician according to
both city newspapers. A graduate of Albany Medical College,
it was Duryee who in 1910 hosted the first state-wide gathering
of mayors for the particular purpose of discussing municipal

health issues. He also worked as a state health commissioner, and throughout his career waged war against tuberculosis, fighting to establish municipal clinics in every major city of the state. He died in 1937 at the age of 78.

By 1912, however, he was done with politics, and in his wake, Sheriff William Hathaway, comptroller Charles Benedict and Schenectady County Democratic Party chairman James C. McDonald all threw their names into the hat. Benedict, with support from Duryee, eventually got the nod. The Republicans, meanwhile, countered with William Herron as their candidate, a General Electric employee who the party tried to sell as "a workingman and a workingman's candidate."

In August, Union-Star reporter William Efner wrote that "Lunn is still the insurgent reformer and nothing more," suggesting that his commitment to the Socialist Party was not all-consuming. While Efner might have been right in the long run about Lunn's devotion to the Socialists, his assessment seemed questionable to most, especially later the following month. In the September 29th issue of The Citizen, just three days after Duryee's announcement that he would not run, the paper ran a huge spread trumpeting the Socialist candidates for most of the city and county offices, and made official what everyone had expected: Lunn would be its candidate for mayor.

"I deeply appreciate the confidence which you have expressed in choosing me to head the Socialist ticket in the coming municipal campaign," said Lunn. "In reality our campaign is a continuous one. The worldwide movement of the producing class to open economic opportunity for all men constitutes a program for continuous work. We do not forget for one moment the ultimate purpose of our movement, but for the next few weeks we will be engaged in a struggle to gain control of our local city government."

The Citizen printed Lunn's acceptance of the nomination in its entirety. Speaking in front of a large assemblage at the Electric Workers Hall on State Street in the Donahue Building, just one door west of the local Socialist headquarters, Lunn went on to say, "The burdens that weigh down upon the backs of the mass of the people will not be lifted by any philanthropic endeavor of individuals, but only by the united effort of the workers themselves will the day ever come when economic emancipation can be realized.

"You workers know well enough that we have in Schenectady the two old parties," continued Lunn. "They have two souls with but a single thought; two hearts that beat as one. They are united in their stand for the present economic system which robs the workers of the fruit of their toil."

In his speech, Lunn reacted to the warnings of the Democrats and Republicans that a Socialist administration would force industry out of the city.

"We know only too well that the development of our home industries is essential to the development of our city and the best welfare of all. The Socialists have never favored any policy that would make the lot of the workers harder and that alone is sufficient answer to these falsehood circulators as to any Socialist warfare against local industries."

In summary, Lunn said; "Let us enter this struggle with confidence not only believing that we will win, but with the knowledge that we will win because we deserve to win. Let us work early and late, night and day, to bring our message to every voter in this city. If we do this, as we will, we may expect on the night of November 7 news that will bring rejoicing to the hearts of the workers not only in this city but throughout the nation. I therefore accept this nomination, deeply grateful for the confidence you have imposed in me."

The city's two daily newspapers wasted little time promoting their candidate. The Schenectady Gazette argued that Benedict, the Democrat, would have a "progressive and economical administration," one which "refuses to make impossible promises," and that would be "free from all entanglements." The Gazette officially endorsed Benedict on October 27, writing that the "people want a chief executive who will govern the city economically." The Union-Star meanwhile, argued that there were "good and sufficient reasons" to elect Herron, and that he alone "has the best interests of the city."

The two Schenectady dailies, while generally complimentary of Lunn and his work in the past, would grow critical of the pastor-turned-politician in the weeks running up to the election. Albany's Knickerbocker Press, meanwhile, which didn't have a horse in the race, produced this description of Lunn from one of its reporters, Douglas K. Miller.

"He is tall, thin, distinguished looking. He has an engaging smile. He jumps from comic to the serious between breaths, forces home arguments with Rooseveltian gestures. He is impetuous, mirthful, has boyish enthusiasm, forces himself into all manner of predicaments and smilingly bluffs his way out." A few weeks later, Miller again wrote about Lunn, telling his readers that "Dr. Lunn was the Socialist nominee for mayor under a special dispensation of the party chiefs, which allowed him to run for office without putting in a two years dues paying apprenticeship. He was never in the novice class in that party."

Although Lunn's popularity soared in 1911, not all of his supporters followed him into the Socialist Party. There was a large group of people called Lunnites who were Democrats and Republicans that were dissatisfied with what the two major parties offered and saw Lunn as a viable alternative. Four years later, as Lunn was parting ways with the Socialists, the term Lunnites was used again to refer to his many supporters during that confrontation. But in October 1911, the increasing number of Lunnites combined with those already registered as Socialists began making the Democrats and Republicans nervous, and both traditional parties began lashing out at Lunn.

At an October 4 meeting of the Schenectady Republican Club, James F. Hooker warned that the General Electric Company would "not appreciate it if Schenectady should elect a Socialist mayor." A New York City native and graduate of Yale University and Columbia Law School, Hooker was President of the Mohawk Clothing Company. He had organized the Progressive Club of the Republican party in Schenectady just a few years earlier, a group that in 1910 would have felt fortunate to secure Lunn as its mayoral candidate.

Schenectady's two major newspapers and The Citizen all reported on Hooker's speech, The Citizen opining that his "implied threat will not have much impact on the voters." While Hooker railed upon the Democrats, including Governor Dix, he also said that the voters should support "even the Democratic ticket" rather than voting for the Socialists, and that the "discordant elements" in his own party, of which he was one, "can be best brought into line and be made to see the necessity of supporting the ticket."

While Hooker and others took the liberty of telling voters how the leaders of GE would feel toward a Lunn victory, in truth they probably didn't have any strong sentiment regarding the election. Lunn and Emmons, GE's General Manager, usually seemed on good terms, and after Lunn had been elected mayor, GE President Charles Coffin was asked for an interview by the anti-Socialist Catholic Magazine and responded by hurrying the reporter out of the office saying, "Dr. Lunn was the best man that had ever been mayor of Schenectady," and Coffin planned to "work hand in glove with him."

There was no scientific polling done in those days, so the favorite in the race for mayor depended upon which newspaper you were reading. All three behaved in the manner of party propaganda publications and suggested that their man was the inevitable victor, the Union-Star being the most blatant with a headline that declared "Herron Wins is General Opinion." The newspaper even reminded its readers in large print that the Republican Party's lineup for the election was row 2 on the ballot. The Gazette, meanwhile, ran huge stories and photos of all the Democratic candidates and made little mention of their opposition. Herron did garner a few headlines, all with negative storylines, while Lunn was practically ignored.

All three parties held rallies the final weekend before the election, but it was clear that the real enthusiasm belonged to the Socialists. One man, reputed to be a prominent Democrat in the city, went to assess Lunn's message at one such rally and found himself leaving before the speech was complete. According to the Utica Globe, when asked why he left early, the man later replied, "I didn't dare stay. Had I remained he would have had me as sure as I'm a foot high, and I would have looked nice yelling for Lunn and holding the positions I do. I tell you he is the greatest campaigner in this state today. He knows how to catch the crowd, hold it, make it understand and see things as he does. I've heard Bryan and Roosevelt, but neither has a thing on Lunn."

On Thursday, November 2, Lunn spoke to a crowd of 4,000 people (some estimates put the number of people at 5,000) at the corner of Paige and Hamilton Streets, and on Friday evening, November 3, Lunn attracted another large throng to the corner of Raymond Street and Avenue B in the Goose Hill section of Schenectady. On Saturday afternoon at 3, he and Herbert Merrill, the Socialist candidate for State Assembly, addressed a gathering at Fischer's Corners in the southwestern section of the city, and that night at 5 p.m. Lunn was speaking again at Crescent Park. Finally, at 8 p.m., Monday, November 6, Lunn made his final campaign speech before a large crowd at Union Station.

His day, however, wasn't yet over with. Later that evening, at 11 p.m., two of Lunn's closest associates in the local Socialist Party, Charles Noonan and Russell Hunt, knocked on Lunn's front door at 16 Jay Street and presented him with a blank resignation form which read in part: "To the end that my official acts may at all times be under the direction and control of the party membership, I hereby sign and place in the hands of local (.....) my resignation to any office to which I may be elected (or appointed), such resignation to become effective whenever a majority of the local shall so vote. I sign this voluntarily as a condition of receiving said nomination, and pledge my honor as a man and Socialist to abide by it."

Nearly nine years later, on January 28, 1920, Lunn testified about his late-night conversation with Noonan and Hunt before a Special Investigative Committee of the New York State Assembly looking into the expulsion of five Socialists from the New York State Legislature.

Lunn remembered that the resignation form "aroused my ire, but I was either to sign it or there would be a squabble the next day. I considered it illegal, but, nevertheless, I did sign it in 1911, once and only."

The polls opened Tuesday, November 7, 1911 at 6 a.m. and closed at 5 p.m. The previous evening the Union-Star reported that enthusiasm for Lunn was fading and that the race was between Herron and Benedict, and that Herron was leading according to an "impartial" poll. Tuesday morning's Gazette, however, declared the race was now between Benedict and Lunn, and that a vote for Herron would be wasted and help elect a Socialist ticket.

The city seemed on edge. The General Electric Company and ALCO were both closed, as were most of the banks and other businesses. But the streets were still crowded with people anxious about the voting. Two of Schenectady's citizens were arrested by police officers simply for trying to vote in the wrong polling place. Even Lunn, who had voted early, was abruptly escorted out of his polling place by an over-zealous official who suggested the candidate was breaking the law by lingering too long and talking to other voters.

A mere 25 minutes after the polling places closed, the Schenectady Illuminating Company, acting on word from the Union-Star, let Schenectady know who was going to be its next mayor. At 5:25 p.m., three flashes of the city's street lights indicated that Lunn was the winner. One flash would have meant success for Benedict, and two would have indicated that Herron was victorious. The Union-Star came out with three separate editions that night and sold 46,240 copies, at the time the most ever by a newspaper in the city.

Lunn won with a total of 6,536 votes. Benedict was next with 4,537, a plurality of 1,999 votes for Lunn, and Herron came in a distant third with 3,954 votes. Lunn carried 18 of the city's 25 election districts, with Benedict claiming six and Herron just one.

The enthusiasm for Lunn and the continuing increase in the city's population accounted for nearly 2,000 more votes cast in 1911 than in 1909. The news of Lunn's victory and the other Socialist successes spread quickly that late Tuesday afternoon, creating a party atmosphere throughout the city that lasted well into the night. Lunn had spent much of the afternoon awaiting election results at Glenn's Hotel and Restaurant at 422 State Street, not more than 100 yards from his home on Jay Street. When it was clear he was going to win, Lunn was herded into an automobile by jubilant supporters and paraded around the city. He headed up to the Christ Episcopal Church at the corner of State and Swan Street in the eastern section of the city and delivered a short speech. He then got back in the automobile with three associates and slowly made his way back downtown, waving to an adoring crowd the whole way. A marching band accompanied Lunn's vehicle and played "La Marseillaise," a song inspired by the French Revolution and later adopted as France's national anthem.

Lunn spoke again briefly at the Socialist party's headquarters on lower State Street, and by 10 p.m. was back at home with his family, where he was greeted by more supporters and a few members of the press. Lunn said he was overjoyed by the victory, especially because so many of his fellow Socialist candidates had also been elected, including eight new city council members, eight county supervisors and Merrill, the first Socialist to earn a seat in the New York state assembly.

"I would have preferred to have been defeated rather than be elected alone," Lunn told a reporter that night.

Lunn's life changed that Tuesday. By Wednesday he had received 129 telegram and phone messages offering congratulations from around the country according to Ralph F. Krueger. The son of Frederick C. Krueger, a city merchant who Lunn would appoint as the first parks commissioner, Ralph was acting as Lunn's "majordomo" reported the Gazette. A resident of 22 Jay Street, within shouting distance of the Lunn home, Krueger was a 21-year-old dental student who was helping Lunn's wife organize all the incoming messages while at the same time trying to keep Lunn's schedule straight for the next few days.

While Lunn and his fellow Socialists were exuberant about the election, the new mayor did extend an olive branch to those who didn't vote for him. A Union-Star headline on Wednesday informed its readers that "Dr. Lunn Promises Not to Tax Industries Away From Schenectady But Rather to Encourage Their Location Here." Lunn also told reporters, "We cannot inaugurate Socialism, but we can show the people what Socialism offers and what Socialist officials can do." According to the Gazette, Herron took his third-place showing well, saying that Lunn was "not dangerous," and while the election outcome, was a surprise, "it is the will of the people, and all we have to do is bow to it."

Lunn gave countless and lengthy interviews to various newspapers from around the state throughout Wednesday and Thursday of election week. He talked about his plans for municipal garbage pickup, how Schenectady should be given "home rule" over its utilities, and how he would continue to speak at the Mohawk Theatre on three Sunday nights each month as pastor of the United People's Church. However, since he "did not believe a man should draw two salaries," he was looking to secure a capable associate who would take over most of the responsibilities connected to the church. As for his duties as editor of The Citizen, Lunn responded, "I will continue to write for the Citizen and will exercise a certain oversight over the policy of the paper. The paper will be published under the direction of a capable managing editor, though. I will act more in an advisory capacity."

On Friday, November 10, exhausted from the election and its aftermath, Lunn and the family headed to Lake George for some rest and relaxation at the home of George Foster Peabody, a wealthy banker and philanthropist. He returned on November 20 and immediately went back to work making plans for his administration. On that night at the Methodist Church, Lunn introduced the Rev. Reginald Campbell, a popular London preacher touring America, and later in the week, on November

23, he officially accepted the oath of office from city clerk John H. Bolan, although he wouldn't assume his duties until January 1, 1912. On Friday, November 24, Lunn and Mayor Duryee met and both parties came away happy with the "half-hour chat," Duryee calling it both "friendly" and "pleasing."

On December 1, Lunn spoke at the Trinity Reformed Church in Amsterdam at the invitation of the Rev. W.N.P. Daily, and on Sunday, December 3, he was in Brooklyn speaking at the Holy Trinity Church. Later that week Lunn delivered an address at the South Broad Street Theatre in Philadelphia, and within the next two weeks spoke at Carnegie Hall in New York City, the University Club in Syracuse, and the Twilight Club in New York City. In Philadelphia, Lunn was asked about the confessions of the McNamara brothers, two young men accused of murder whose defense had been supported by the Socialist Party in California. "The confessions to me, as they were to a million other workmen, were a big shock," responded Lunn. "Before the confessions I thought that the manner in which the McNamaras were kidnapped by Detective Burns was illegal. Apparently, the two men were as guilty as sin. If the Socialist candidate knew they were guilty and aided their cause, he deserves to lose because no party has a right to build its foundations on fraud."

Lunn went on to speak at Boston and Rochester during December, and on December 21 he was at Bleecker Hall in Albany. After a brief respite for the holidays, on December 29 Lunn joined Merrill, Victor Berger and Morris Hillquist at the Grove Street studio of Miss Helen Stokes in New York City for the third annual meeting of the Inter-Collegiate Socialist Society. Stokes, a painter, was a popular "parlor Socialist," the term referring to someone who supported socialism regardless of their great individual wealth. The next day, December 30, Lunn was back in Schenectady Saturday afternoon making final preparations to assume power on Monday morning.

1911 had drawn to a close and it had been an eventful year. Around the world, Italy had declared war on the Ottoman Empire, Norwegian Roald Amundsen had reached the South

Pole, and a former Louvre employee named Vicenzo Perugia had stolen the Mona Lisa (it was returned in 1914). President William Howard Taft had sent troops to the Texas and New Mexico borders to keep the violence of the Mexican Revolution from spilling into the U.S., a Native American named Ishi was the last of his people to make contact with European-Americans, Ty Cobb won his fourth batting title with an average of .420, and the Philadelphia Athletics defeated the New York Giants in the World Series in six games.

Schenectady, meanwhile, just a small city on the Mohawk River two decades earlier, was now bursting at the seams and developing its reputation as "the city that lights and hauls the world." It was also a city at the forefront of a worker's movement that, although falling short of its political goals, would make great strides on behalf of the working class in the first half of the 20th century.

CHAPTER 10

Taking Office

"Never before has Schenectady ushered into office an executive with greater enthusiasm than was accorded Dr. George R. Lunn as mayor."
Schenectady Gazette, January 2, 1912.

On Saturday night, December 30, after receiving a solid gold watch from his friends in the Democratic party, exiting mayor Charles Duryee dispatched a messenger from his home at 1352 Union St. to 16 North Jay St., the home of George Lunn. With the messenger were the keys to City Hall.

On Monday morning, January 1, Lunn showed up at 8 a.m. and City Clerk John H. Bolan, soon to be replaced by devout Socialist Hawley Van Vechten, was there waiting for him. Lunn's executive secretary was Walter Lippmann, who would become the most influential newspaperman in the first half of the 20th century. Lippmann had met Lunn a few weeks earlier at a meeting arranged by New York City Socialist Morris Hillquist, and the recent Harvard grad was at his new post at 8:30 that morning, excited to be a part of the Socialist experiment in Schenectady. "We are having desk lights fixed because this administration intends to work night as well as day," Lippmann told the Union-Star. "The previous rulers do not seem to have had that practice." What would be a very long day for Lunn was under way.

There was no inaugural ceremony, Lunn having officially been sworn in on November 23, but there were plenty of meet-and-greets, happy handshakes, and short, off-the-cuff speeches. Socialist officials from all over upstate New York were among the 2,000 or so supporters surrounding City Hall who just wanted to be a part of the action. Helen Stokes, who had hosted Lunn just a few days earlier in New York City was there, as was Miss Mary R. Sanford, a young woman who had worked with Lippmann on the Intercollegiate Socialist Society while they were both at Harvard two years earlier. Charles Mullen, who Lunn recruited from Milwaukee to serve as Commissioner of Public Works, and Walter E. Kruesi, a former Schenectady resident who had moved to Boston before being selected by Lunn to become the new Commissioner of Charities, both were there. So was Russell Hunt, the new president of the Common Council who would oversee a group of eight Socialists, three Democrats, two Republicans, and Charles Noonan, who along with Hunt had visited Lunn prior to election night back in November to remind him where his priorities should be. Noonan's celebrating was perhaps a bit subdued since his victory as Seventh Ward alderman was being contested by Omar E. De La Mater, the incumbent he had replaced. A Republican, De La Mater didn't argue that Noonan was ineligible to hold office, but that he was ineligible to vote. Canadian by birth, having been born in Melrose, New Brunswick, Noonan came to Schenectady to work for the GE in 1895, and served in the U.S. Army during the Spanish-American War. The issue of eligibility was decided in Noonan's favor by a court later in the month.

Lunn's first week as mayor was a busy one, dominated by well wishers offering congratulations and his efforts to end the strike at ALCO. Following his dramatic confrontation with Captain Bowen at 6:30 that Wednesday morning, January 3, Lunn was back at the plant 90 minutes later. accompanied by the Commissioner of Public Safety John E. Cole and the health officer, William P. Faust. They were greeted by plant manager John R. Magarvey and other ALCO officials, along with Captain Bowen who apologized for not recognizing Lunn at their first meeting. This meeting, referred to as a "tour" of the plant, went without incident. Lunn met with ALCO Vice-President James McNaughton and other officials three days later, on a Saturday, to discuss the strike, giving them ample opportunity to debrief the mayor on exactly what the strike was all about – at least their version of it.

"The interview with the mayor was of a most friendly nature and has afforded me a much desired opportunity to fully explain to him the company's position in the matter," McNaughton told the press after Lunn had left. "The mayor manifested great interest in what I had to say and now has full knowledge of all the circumstances leading up to and attending the strike." When Lunn met with reporters later Saturday he said that his conference with McNaughton had been a pleasant one, and that "the outlook is decidedly encouraging."

Lunn's first weekend on the job was a busy one. On Sunday night, he headed north about 20 miles to Ballston Spa and spoke to a standing-room-only crowd at the Elite Theater. He told the audience how "socialism prevents the rich man from taking what the workingman produces. Rocky [Rockefeller], Carnegie and Morgan may not be to blame for the present condition of affairs, but they are working the system for all it is worth." Lunn went on to say that "Lincoln would not be tolerated in the Republican Party today," and that "while Roosevelt wants to save the Grand Old Party, I say away with it, down with it."

The Gazette reported that the "Elite Theatre did not begin to accommodate the crowd which came this afternoon to hear Mayor George. R. Lunn of Schenectady talk on socialism." Also, while large crowds at such gatherings were not unusual, there was something different about this one. "Curiosity," wrote the Gazette, helped bring out a large crowd, "many of whom were women."

Around the same time Lunn was speaking in Ballston Spa that Sunday night, two other "progressive" politicians had a chance meeting at Union Station in Washington, D.C. that made headlines in newspapers all over the country. William Jennings Bryan, the leader of the liberal faction of the Democratic Party, and U.S. Senator Bob LaFollette of Wisconsin, Bryan's counterpart in the Republican Party, ran into each other when their trains just happened to come into D.C. at the same time. "They rushed toward each other and shook hands and then lost no time in withdrawing a short distance from the crowd," according to newspaper accounts, "where they conversed with evident earnestness for several minutes."

When Progressives of all stripes heard of the meeting, talk of a third-party ticket for the presidency with Bryan and LaFollette was inevitable and exciting but not very realistic. Both men downplayed their brief chat, and insisted their conversation was solely about the issue of the popular vote for senatorial candidates, something also trumpeted by Lunn until the law was finally passed as the 17th Amendment in 1913. Lunn no doubt read the Associated Press article in the Gazette that day about the Bryan-LaFollette meeting, but he also noticed another headline commenting on his upcoming address to the Schenectady Common Council later that Monday night. "There is much speculation as to what the message will contain," the Gazette said of Lunn's first official address as mayor, "but it is sure to be brim full of oratorical pyrotechnics."

At 8 p.m. Monday, January 8, the new mayor walked into the City Hall Annex and read his first message to the citizens of Schenectady, officially laying out his plans to make life better for everyone in the city, not just the rich. It was a long speech, filled with lofty rhetoric praising socialism and decrying capitalism, and there were also plenty of details; a laundry list of just what his goals were and how he would go about reaching them. He immediately addressed the minority faction of the city council, the three Democrats and two Republicans that weren't swept aside by the Socialist victory. Throughout Lunn's first two-year term, those five would typically vote as a block in opposition to whatever the mayor and the eight Socialists on the council would push forward.

"While we hope to be aided, not hindered by this minority," he said, "we all know that the Socialists alone will be held strictly accountable for the honest and efficient conduct of city affairs. We assume that responsibility with confidence."

Lunn boldly said that he and other Socialists "would abolish the capitalist system with its whole retinue of social evils," if they could, but that power wasn't yet within their grasps. "What we can do, however, is to take advantage of the glorious opportunity open to the Socialists of Schenectady of demonstrating to the people of this city and the country at large the spirit of socialism and the application of socialist principles so far as that is possible under the handicap of laws framed to establish and sustain the capitalist system."

Lunn cited the muckraking press for exposing the corruption so prevalent in government at that time, but he added that "exposure is the merest beginning – with it we clear the ground for the work of construction.... we are prepared to build anew where the old stood."

In his address, Lunn stated that initially he had five major goals:

No. 1 – We must guard and promote the health of the community.

No. 2 – We must enlarge the scope of education until it includes men and women in a continued process of increasing enlightenment.

No. 3 – We must do what we can to establish economic security.

No. 4 – We must have efficiency clearly distinguished from red tape.

No. 5 – We must have true economy – a thing which is not the equivalent of mere expense cutting.

Lunn went on to specifically mention the fight to eliminate tuberculosis, the upgrading of the milk inspection process, the building of city parks and playgrounds, and the importance of improving the educational opportunities. He also argued for the public ownership of all utilities, a public market, and municipal garbage collection.

"We look upon government.... not as an adjunct to private business," he summed up. "For us, government is the instrument through which wrong can be righted, poverty abolished, life made secure, cities healthful, citizens happy. It will cease to be the weapon of property in order to become the instrument through which the people can make cities worthy of human life."

Lunn traveled to New York City to meet with Socialist officials on Tuesday, but was back in Schenectady by Wednesday night, preparing for a visit from the Socialist mayor of Milwaukee, Emil Seidel. Also on the rails to Schenectady was Joseph Franklin, President of the International Brotherhood of Boilermakers, leading Lunn to believe that the strike would be over by the end of the week. He was right. While Lunn, Seidel, Morris Hillquist and Henry Bruere, Director of the Bureau of Municipal Research, were talking about putting socialism into action, Franklin announced at noon on Friday that the strike at ALCO was over. It had started ten weeks earlier on October 26 in support of striking railroad workers at New York Central in New York City. Saturday night's Schenectady Press Club dinner, with Lunn and Seidel the guests of honor, must have been an upbeat affair. While the strike hadn't ended on great terms for the workers, many of the men would be working by Monday. As for Henry Bowen, captain of the company guards, he left Schenectady that Saturday night and headed east on a train for Boston where a longshoremen's strike had begun on January 5. Six weeks later, with Bowen's help, the bosses had crushed the union and ended the strike with no gains for the workers.

While the activities of the new Socialist administration and the ALCO strike dominated the first two weeks of January 1912, there was other news going on that month. The Rev. Robert Bakeman arrived from East Jefferson, N.H., in the third week of January after being appointed assistant pastor at the United People's Church, allowing Lunn to concentrate on politics. On January 22, Sergeant Bath, the police officer who had come to Lunn's rescue on the Front Street bridge on Jan. 3, arrested four women in a raid at Franklin and South Centre Street for violating an ordinance that "prohibits gathering of women in saloons or apartments for immoral purposes." Later that week at the Schenectady library, Mrs. Rose Perkins Hale and Mrs. Harriet Stanton Blatch, two prominent suffragates, led a large gathering of women seeking the right to vote. Two weeks later on January 26, 500 individuals paid $3 apiece to watch cock-fights in Hoffman's, a small Schenectady County settlement on the Mohawk River just a few miles west of the city. Police eventually broke up the event.

The night before at the Albany YMCA, Lunn spoke to 500 people, telling them that "socialism is the greatest moral movement of our time," and that "we Americans are being stirred on these great economic and industrial questions, as we have never been before in our history. "Lunn, who also criticized the efforts of both President Taft and Teddy Roosevelt, stated that "there is no essential difference" between socialism and Christianity.

On January 29th, a Monday, Lunn testified on behalf of Noonan in his fight to retain the city council seat he won in November, and on Wednesday Schenectady County sized up its political landscape, announcing that among its voting population, 5,916 were Republicans, 3,851 were Democrats, and 2,023 were Socialists. How many of those 2,023 registered Socialists were at the Mohawk Club, a bastion of the city's economic elite, the night before is unknown, but an event called the "Made in Schenectady" dinner attracted 300 prominent citizens dedicated to upgrading the prospects of the city's business outlook. The mayor was not one of them. Organized by the Board of Trades and its secretary, Walter H. Reed, the group listened to an advertising executive from New York City, Herbert Durand, tell them how to best lure entrepreneurs and their businesses to Schenectady.

"Do not hide your light under a bushel," said Durand, paraphrasing the words of Matthew, Chapter 5:15. "The prime purpose of this getting together of optimists is, I take it, to find a way to let the new light of Old Dorp so shine before men that they may see your good works and skedaddle hither to share in them and magnify them." Durand stressed advertising, and another speaker, N.I. Schermerhorn, a former Board of Trades president, suggested that the city's new administration should include in its budget a "publicity fund." The idea elicited great roars of approval from those on hand.

On Tuesday, when the Union-Star's Albany correspondent approached Herbert Merrill in the State Assembly, the Schenectady Socialist felt the idea had plenty of merit. "It is what other cities are compelled to do under present conditions, and Schenectady should not be behind," said Merrill. "If the administration of a city wants an enabling act so that the budget may carry an allowance for the Board of Trade publicity plan, I shall gladly do my part toward obtaining the necessary legislation."

When that same correspondent also found Lunn in Albany on Wednesday, the mayor wasn't so sure. He thought that $10,000 was too much to give to the advertising fund, but declined to offer any more judgement on the idea, telling the reporter he would have to think about it some more.

Thursday morning's Gazette produced a more complete response from Lunn, which certainly must have disappointed the Board of Trades. While he didn't totally discard the idea, he didn't give it his hearty endorsement.

"It would be a good thing for all concerned if we could bring to Schenectady one or more industries which could be operated here to better advantage than where they are now located, in regard to their extension and development," said Lunn. "But it is difficult how anyone would desire to take industry from other cities to bring them here for selfish purposes."

Lunn spent the first week of February in Albany pushing for "home rule," which referred to legislation that would allow municipalities to choose their department heads and other employees in the way they thought best. On February 12, Lincoln's birthday, he travelled to Cambridge, Massachusetts and spoke before the Harvard Socialist Club, telling them that "the present system of extracting profits and therefore failing to make fair exchange makes us stand for a system of robbery. We have no right to take profit from the worker until it is to be reinvested for the public good." Lunn's trip east allowed him to spend part of the day in Lawrence, Massachusetts, where striking textile workers gave him some indication of the kind of trouble he would experience later that year in Little Falls.

"I came to Lawrence this morning to see the Civil War that is in existence here, and the conditions are as abominable as could be imagined," Lunn told striking workers at Needham Hall. After reminding the strikers that the day was Lincoln's birthday, he then quoted the 16th President, saying, "Labor is prior to capital. Capital is the fruit of labor. Capital could not have existed had not labor first existed. Labor is superior to capital and deserves much higher consideration."

The workers' grievances in the Lawrence textile mills made what Lunn dealt with at the ALCO plant a month earlier look trivial. At capacity, the major mills in Lawrence employed 32,000 men, women and children. At one mill, more than 50 percent of the workers were teenage girls between 14 and 18. At other plants about half of the workers were women, nearly all of them unskilled immigrants. The mortality rate for children living in Lawrence's slums was 50 percent by age 6, and 36 out of every 100 men, women and children who worked at the mill were dead by the time they reached their mid 20s. Things reached a boil on January 1, 1912, when a new Massachusetts law went into effect restricting the number of hours a company could force women and children to work. A two-hour deduction from a 56 to 54-hour work week was too much for the corporate chiefs to bear, so while they complied with the law they significantly cut the workers' wages. On January 11, female Polish weavers at one mill shut down their looms and left for home, and within a week more than 20,000 others had joined them.

"We want bread, but roses too," became the rallying cry, the motto indicating that the strikers not only wanted a pay raise, but also some respect.

By March 12, with the help of the IWW and Arturo Giovannitti of the Italian Socialist Federation of the Socialist Party of

America, the strike was settled with the workers making some small gains. As in the Little Falls strike later that year, where workers sent their young ones to Schenectady, some of the Lawrence children were sent to foster homes in New York City. Also, just a few days before Lunn arrived, Anna LoPizzo, a striking worker, was killed as police broke up a picket line. While the strikers accused the police of shooting LoPizzo, the authorities arrested Giovannitti and IWW leader Joseph Ettor and charged them as accessories in the woman's death. Both men were actually three miles away from the incident at a public meeting. All of the incidents surrounding the strike were gaining national attention, and with the workers on the receiving end of more and more public sympathy, the mill bosses eventually relented and made some minor concessions.

Lunn only spent part of one day in Lawrence, but it must have felt like he had travelled to some distant country, or even another world. On his return to Schenectady that night, Lunn was met by the local press as he got off the train. "Mayor, how would you like to be mayor of Lawrence?" asked one of the reporters, to which Lunn replied, "I am glad I live in Schenectady and in New York State."

Two weeks after Lunn's speech at Harvard, the university decided to ban all controversial oratory on campus. In 1911, the school's leaders, in an attempt to block a speech by British suffragate Emmeline Pankhurst, had ruled that women could not speak on campus unless they were invited by "the corporation." As for Lunn and others like him, Harvard declared "That the halls of the university shall not be open to persistent or sympathetic propaganda on contentious questions of contemporaneous social, economic, political or religious interests."

CHAPTER 11

Steinmetz Joins the Team

While Lunn's popularity was reaching new heights early in his first term, nothing he ever did was received with more universal acclaim than his appointment of Dr. Charles Proteus Steinmetz to the Schenectady School Board on February 29. Born in Breslau, Germany on April 5, 1865, Steinmetz was a mathematician and electrical engineer who, since coming to the General Electric Company in 1894, had won the hearts and minds of nearly all Schenectadians. A World War with his native homeland a few years in the future and his isolationist views leading up to that conflict cooled some of the warm feeling directed Steinmetz's way, but only for a short time, and in 1912 he was as beloved a figure as you could find.

Despite his appearance – he suffered from dwarfism, hunchback and hip dysplasia – and some initial shyness because of it, Steinmetz made friends with relative ease in Schenectady, as he had done in Yonkers when he first came to this country in 1889. Not quite five feet tall, Steinmetz never completed his doctorate at the University of Breslau or the Swiss Federal Polytechnic Institute, but there was no disputing his genius. Within five years after disembarking at Castle Garden (three years before Ellis Island opened) and nearly being put back on a boat, Steinmetz landed a position with General Electric – Thomas Edison's company – and before he died in 1923 his name and fame would put him on equal footing with the likes of Einstein, Ford, Marconi, Tesla, Westinghouse, and even Edison himself.

When Lunn was elected mayor in November 1911, he and Steinmetz were not close. Steinmetz's activities with the student Socialist Club at Breslau – not a favorite of the Bismarck administration – led to his exit from Germany back in 1888, but since coming to America he had kept a low profile in political matters.

But when Lunn and the Socialists assumed power in Schenectady, Steinmetz contacted the new mayor and offered to help in any way he could. Along with the good publicity that he brought to Schenectady as the "Wizard of GE" and the "Modern Jupiter," Steinmetz had also created Union College's Engineering Department in 1904 and was even more popular on campus then he was in the city. His students adored him, and one fraternity actually invited him to join, a rare distinction for a member of the faculty. Along with providing him with the title of professor, the Union hierarchy also awarded him an honorary doctorate. If all his scientific knowledge and enthusiasm for education wasn't enough to endear him to everyone, Steinmetz was also extremely polite, honest and approachable to all who crossed his path, particularly children. There is the anecdotal story of how one night Steinmetz was visited at his home by Henry Ford, who was looking for a way to make his cars run more efficiently. Steinmetz told Ford he would be happy to help, but he first had to spend some time reading to his adopted grandchildren as he had promised. Ford, the story goes, spent the next hour walking the streets of Schenectady waiting for Steinmetz to finish his grandfatherly obligations.

Lunn was quite happy to receive Steinmetz's help, and he quickly appointed him to the school board. At the first meeting of the new group on March 13, Steinmetz, who got there 15 minutes late, was elected president by his fellow board members.

"Gentlemen, I feel the honor greatly," Steinmetz told the board. "For years I have been interested in educational matters. Nevertheless, I would hesitate to undertake such work if I could not feel confident I would have your assistance, especially of you members who have continued on the board."

Joining Steinmetz as new members of the board were William McTaggert, a progressive Republican and a foreman at GE, and Henry W. Gould, a Socialist and iron worker at GE. The two holdovers Steinmetz thanked for staying on were Duryee appointees Clement W. Bailey, a Democrat, and John Diehl, a Republican. The Gazette, not a big Lunn supporter by any means, applauded the choice of Steinmetz.

"Dr. Steinmetz is a man of force of character and remarkable intellectual ability," said the newspaper. "His affiliation with the board of education places at the disposal of the city the brains of a man whose intellectual as well as practical training has been unusual."

About the only people who had some reservations about Steinmetz's selection were staunch Socialists. After all, he lived in the GE Realty Plot with a number of other wealthy company executives, he hadn't yet joined the local Socialist party, and he had been a registered Republican since voting in his first municipal election in Schenectady in 1894 after becoming a U.S. citizen. Some may have wondered just how devoted to the Socialist effort Steinmetz was, but in August of that year he quieted most dissenters by finally joining the local and becoming a close ally of Lunn's.

The two were a great team. The city's school system grew into something that better handled Schenectady's rapid population growth, and the creation of a number of parks and playgrounds by the city government, particularly Central Park along the eastern edge of the city, offered residents a welcome escape from their urban existence.

While the mayor was quite happy to have Steinmetz on the team in 1912, he was also rather pleased with the makeup of his school board, except for one thing.

"The city is indeed fortunate in securing the services of these men. [But] it is a disappointment to me that I was unable to name a woman as a member." Two weeks later, however, some hard work by Lunn's Schenectady comrade in the state assembly paved the way for women to become eligible to serve in municipal posts throughout New York. "I am glad that the first legislation introduced by assemblyman Merrill to pass the legislature is in favor of the rights of women. We stand out and for woman suffrage, and if we did not we would not seek to appoint a woman to the Board of Education."

Two days before he named Steinmetz to the school board, Lunn announced his plans for a social welfare board, and on

March 11 the city council voted to support his proposal. "The election of last November was a mandate from the people of Schenectady that a new era has begun," said Lunn. "It was a straightforward announcement that government must cease to be the agent of private business in order to become an instrument for human welfare."

The board would include the mayor himself, the president of the common council, president of the bureau of health, superintendant of schools, commissioner of public works, and two others appointed by the mayor.

But, as popular as Lunn was and as successful as he seemed getting many of his ideas initiated, not everything went well. On February 7, a day after Lunn overruled a city ordinance prohibiting "coasting" on city streets, an 11-year-old girl, Gladys Dwyer, was fatally injured in an accident on Division Street when the sled she was riding smashed into a large horse-drawn wagon driven by city employee Matthew Ball. While Ball, who failed to heed a warning to stop by other children in the area, was arrested and nearly indicted for manslaughter, Lunn was hearing it from both the Gazette and Union-Star. Still mouth pieces for the two other political parties in town, the two newspapers questioned Lunn's authority to nullify a city ordinance simply on his demand, the Union-Star going as far as calling him a dictator. But the furor over the accident eventually died down when the Dwyer family welcomed Lunn at the girl's funeral and a few days later the grand jury cleared Ball of any legal wrongdoing.

Then, the day after the sledding accident, Socialists in the city administration announced, with Lunn's hearty endorsement, that two special courses, "economic theories" and "philosophy of history" would be taught at the high school. However, the idea of a "School of Socialism" immediately produced a lot of negative feedback from the community, catching Lunn totally by surprise.

"You would think from these reports that the Socialists were going to teach Socialism instead of arithmetic to school children," Lunn told the Union Star. "Nothing is further from our minds.

"What we are planning to do is to give Schenectady what it has long needed – a study class in which grown men and women can study economics and social science and fit themselves for intelligent citizenship. The class has been started by the Socialists. If they are fit to govern a city, I guess they are fit to start a class in the study of government for those who care to learn."

Lunn, however, realized he was fighting a losing battle. He later said that the proposal was not well named and suggested that the initial announcement included a few errors. Rev. Dr. Taylor of St. George's Church came out against the idea, and Rev. Henry H. Murdock, president of the Schenectady Ministerial Association said, "I think the attempt to use the public schools as places for advancing the Socialist propaganda is ill advised and is sure to meet with opposition. If the Socialists desire to advance their peculiar political interests there are buildings enough they can secure for this purpose. Hands off the public school for sectarian or political purposes is my motto."

Another embarrassing situation for the mayor arose during the first week of March when the Union-Star reported that in 1910, according to Democratic leader John F. Kileen, Lunn had agreed to run for congress as a Democrat. The agreement between Kileen and Lunn happened just a short time before Lunn officially joined the local Socialist Party, and the nomination never occurred because too many Schenectady Democrats were against it.

Lunn downplayed the report, suggesting that most people in the know were already aware that some Democrats in 1910, as well as some Republicans, were trying to get Lunn on their ticket.

"That is ancient history as your paper said," Lunn told a Union-Star reporter. "My connection with a probable Democratic congressional nomination was generally known during the last campaign and I referred to it myself in some of my speeches. But the facts are these: There was at the time indicated a movement on foot among radical members of the Democratic Party to take a stand against the old order of things, and these radical Democrats were after me to run for congress. As I recall the matter now, if the radical Democrats had gained ascendancy, I might have fallen into the trap so skillfully laid by my dear Democratic friends. But whether I would have accepted a nomination or not is now a thing of the past.

"All this was at a time when I believed that a newspaper could be run as an independent paper, and The Citizen was so run then," continued Lunn. "When I joined the Socialist Party, I cut off all relationship with and faith in the old parties. The Citizen became a partisan paper. There is no paper published today that is not partisan, and there is no individual interested in politics who is not a partisan."

Also, before the winter of 1911-1912 was over, Lunn would receive a handful of death threats and deal with plenty of infighting within the Socialist local, much of the discontent aimed at him. One death threat, a "Black Hand" letter used by the Italian mafia in New York City around the turn of the century, told Lunn to "lower the taxes and put the men that apply for work to work or if you don't you will be no more." Lunn shared the letter with police, but the author was never apprehended.

As for Lunn's fellow Socialists in Schenectady, the group was already split into different chapters: English, German, Polish and Italian. On the night of March 14, the Germans seemed particularly upset with Lunn, questioning many of his appointments in key positions, including John Cole, public safety commissioner, and John F. Millington, a clerk in the health department and milk inspector. Both men were non-Socialists, and while Lunn conceded that some of Cole's appointments had been suspect, he wasn't disappointed with his work. Some of the Germans actually heckled Lunn during the meeting and threatened to use his written resignation against him. At the English meeting that same night, Lunn handled angry questions from both City Council President Russell Hunt and Seventh Ward Alderman Charles Noonan, the two men that had presented Lunn with that resignation form on the eve of election night. The Gazette wrote that Noonan, the man who had created the party in Schenectady County just a few years earlier, "was disappointed when he saw Dr. Lunn elected to a $3,500 a year job, while he had to be content with a $500 one."

Lunn wasn't the only one dealing with complaints. There was also a motion to threaten Merrill with his pre-written resignation if he didn't support a bill in the State Assembly that would allow saloons to be open on Sundays from 2-10 p.m. Merrill sent word that he favored the bill but was hoping to write his own legislation on the matter, a response that did not sit well with many members at the meeting. The interests of those wishing to have a drink on Sunday were of no concern to Lunn. He made his lack of sympathy clear, telling his colleagues that "the liquor traffic is the most despicable business in which a man can engage, and of all the persons in it about 90 percent can be classed as divekeepers and immoral characters."

On the state-wide front, incumbent president William Howard Taft won the New York Republican primary on March 26 over his predecessor in the White House, Theodore Roosevelt, and Wisconsin progressive Robert LaFollette. It was the first primary in New York history, delegates to the national convention having previously been selected at a state-wide gathering, and the logistics were a nightmare. "Big Confusion Throughout the City," blared the New York Tribune, while the Sun proclaimed, "Kings, Queens and Richmond Largely Disenfranchised." There were enough problems, the big one being a lack of ballots, that Roosevelt supporters were able to cry foul, and while Tammany Hall, which backed Taft, was pleased with the process, the New York Times wrote, "the primary election here today was not only a farce, but goes beyond that and is an insult to the city."

On Tuesday, April 2, Schenectady Socialists looked to the Midwest and kept a close eye on the city and county-wide elections in Milwaukee, Wisconsin. The news was not good. What had been such a great victory two years ago when Emil Seidel became the first Socialist mayor of a major city in the U.S., was now another failed experiment in Socialist rule. A fusion ticket of the Democrats and Republicans had beaten Seidel as well as all the other Socialists who had won the 1910 elections for alderman and county supervisors. Gerhard Adolph Bading, a physician and Milwaukee's health commissioner from 1906-1910, became the mayor with 43,000 votes to Seidel's 30,000, and won again in 1914 before too much partisan bickering signaled the demise of Milwaukee's non-partisan political success. Later that summer Seidel ran as Debs' vice-presidential candidate. but that defeat proved to be the zenith of his political career. He did run for the U.S. Senate in 1932 and won just six percent of the vote, but for the most part his political sphere remained on the local level, winning two terms as a Milwaukee alderman in 1916 and 1932. Socialists would return to the mayor's office in Milwaukee, but never enjoyed the same city-wide success that swept Seidel and eight other Socialists into office in 1910. Six years later Dan Hoan became mayor and would serve in that capacity for 20 years, the longest tenure ever for a Socialist mayor. And, in 1948, another Socialist, Frank Zeidler would win the mayor's office and serve until 1960. Both men, while extolling socialism's virtues, were moderates who throughout their careers battled with city councils controlled by one of the two traditional parties.

Meanwhile, Woodrow Wilson, a college professor from Princeton and Governor of New Jersey, was speaking in Buffalo on April 10 while campaigning for the Democratic nomination, telling his audience there that "socialism's rise is due to the disappointment of voters in the two major parties."

CHAPTER 12

Lippmann Exits

Walter Lippmann always had something to say. For more than half a century - from World War I through the war in Vietnam – he shared his thoughts with the American public and they listened, or more precisely, they read and absorbed what he had to say. His magazine articles and newspaper columns made him the most influential American writer of his day according to most historians, and no one can begin to match his longevity. Lippmann helped Woodrow Wilson verbalize his plan for peace following World War I, and in the 1960s he urged Lyndon Baines Johnson to get the U.S. out of Vietnam.

Lippmann was born in New York City on September 23, 1889, and graduated from Harvard in 1910. His classmates included fellow Socialists and journalists John Silas "Jack" Reed and Heywood Broun, as well as playwright, poet and social critic T.S. Eliot. A likable young man who was always impressing his elders, Lippmann helped create the Harvard Socialist Club while also serving as editor of the Harvard Monthly. In 1911, muckraking journalist Lincoln Steffens hired Lippmann to help him at "Everybody's Magazine," and described him as "keen, quiet, industrious, he understood the meaning of all that he learned."

In his 1999 book, "Walter Lippmann and the American Century," Ronald Steel wrote: "What attracted Lippmann to socialism was not a fiery passion for justice and equality, as was the case with his friend John Reed, but an impatience with how badly society was managed."

Steel also suggested that Lippmann wasn't liked by everyone he crossed paths with, writing that Lippmann "was gregarious to a fault, although he was prone to a form of self-aggrandizement that did not sit well with many of his high-minded progressive allies." And, when Lippmann came into conflict with someone, according to Steel, he "defended himself by casting the offending person from his life."

But in December 1911 when he first met Lunn, Lippmann was just 22, a socialist, and, as far as his circle of friends could see, destined for greatness. After being introduced to Lunn in New York City by Morris Hillquist, Lippmann was thrilled to have the opportunity to come to Schenectady for the "great socialist experiment." It's impossible to say just when Lippmann started souring on practical politics, but on April 18th, Lippmann announced his resignation as the mayor's executive secretary, and said only that he planned to devote more time to magazine work and a summer-long book project.

"I deeply regret that the demands of my work make it impossible for me to continue my residence in Schenectady," Lippmann wrote in his letter of resignation, which would take effect May 1. "For this reason, I am offering you my resignation from the position of executive secretary."

Lunn accepted the registration and responded with a written reply to Lippmann. "Your work as executive secretary has been so completely satisfactory that I accept your resignation with unqualified regret, understanding as I do the necessity for your residence in New York City. I want you to know that I shall always appreciate the splendid service you have rendered the city."

While the parting gave every impression of being a harmonious one, it doesn't seem possible that Lunn could have been totally unaware of Lippmann's disappointment in the mayor and his administration. A couple of months later, in a letter to English socialist Graham Wallas, Lippmann said, "I fought as hard as I could within the organization without any result. When I saw that the policy and program were settled, I resigned and attacked the administration."

His attack came on June 9 in the form of an essay in the New York Call, New York City's socialist newspaper, entitled "Schenectady the Unripe." Citing a "timidity of action," and "the lack of a bold plan," Lippmann said that he resigned, "believing there were more important things to do than to take part in 'good gov-

ernment politics.'" Lippmann wrote that "Schenectady Socialism is what happens when we turn from education to politics,
when we seek to win votes rather than to make converts."

As for Lunn, Lippmann described him as a "great spellbind-
er, resourceful, he knows that attack is the only defense." But he
also suggested that it was "hard to learn in the rush of office,"
and he was disappointed in Lunn's list of appointees to the administration. "We need not just good doctors and lawyers," wrote
Lippman, "but doctors and lawyers that are socialists." Lippman
added, "I had no history and no future in Schenectady. It was a
job to do and an experiment to watch."

Lunn offered no public response to Lippmann's critique,
and instead relinquished the job of rebutting Lippmann's article
to Hillquist, who had been acting as the administration's counsel. On June 14, however, Lippmann headed to Schenectady for
an hour-long meeting with Lunn. While the younger man may
have been disappointed in the 38-year-old mayor, the only plau-
sible reason for this meeting is that Lippmann hoped, to some
degree, to smooth the waters between he and Lunn. Both men
refused to comment on their private conversation in Lunn's
office, but according to the Gazette, "both Mr. Lippmann and
the mayor permitted the newspaperman to leave with the impression that the conference had been an amicable one."

Lippmann told the Gazette that he had stopped in Albany,
on his way by train from New York City to Harvard's commencement the next day, and had come to Schenectady in an automobile to see Lunn. He had not been "summoned, nor had he
come to explain." He had, however, according to the Gazette
report, "expected his article would cause hard feelings in certain
quarters among Socialists." When Lippmann had jumped back
in the automobile for the drive back to Albany and his train east,
Lunn told reporters that his young ex-secretary was a member
of that faction of the Socialist Party called the "impossibles," a
group according to Lunn that did not believe in any kind of
reform administration, and felt that a Socialist administration
should have a "stamp of socialism, and socialism alone." Lunn

also let it be known that Lippmann had originally informed him that he was going to write an article for The Call, and that he had hoped to let Lunn see it before it was published.

When reporters pressed Lunn about Lippmann "taking advantage of his confidential position in the administration to rush into print," he didn't take the bait. Instead, "Lunn tried his best to appear unconcerned and unruffled by the criticism of the former secretary," reported the Gazette. "He repeatedly emphasized the fact that he and Mr. Lippmann had always been the best of friends, and that friendship still existed."

A few weeks after his visit in Schenectady, Lippmann left his parents' house in New York City and headed to the Rangeley Lakes region of Maine. Armed with a "splendid little collection of letters informing me that I have 'botched' my political career," Lippmann went off to write a book about politics. A Harvard friend, Alfred Booth Kuttner, agreed to accompany Lippmann, also having a book issue on his calendar. Kuttner would spend the next few months translating Freud's classic, "Interpretation of Dreams," while Lippmann produced "A Preface to Politics," a work that would catapult the 23-year-old into the national spotlight. Lippmann, who had left Schenectady because Lunn and his administration weren't good enough Socialists, walked out of the Maine woods a different man than the one that walked in. He was no longer a Socialist, and in his new book, published in 1913, Lippmann attacked all kinds of progressivism as well as human nature. "Tammany" he wrote, referring to New York City's corrupt political machine, "has a better perception of human need, and comes nearer to being what a government should be, than any scheme yet proposed by a group of 'uptown good government' reformers. " The book received glowing reviews, helping Lippmann and two colleagues start up a new magazine, "The New Republic," in 1914.

Lippman's move toward the political center was so fast that in the fall of 1912, just a few weeks after exiting the Maine woods, he had already forsaken socialism and would vote for Republican candidate Theodore Roosevelt in the November presidential election instead of Socialist candidate Eugene Debs. By 1916, Lippmann was continuing to evolve and voted to re-elect president Woodrow Wilson, who offered him a job in the administration as assistant to Secretary of War Newton Baker. "It is of more far-reaching importance that men should become liberal-minded than that they should believe in a radical creed," Lippman had written back in the fall of 1912.

During World War I, Lippman went to France as a military intelligence officer and helped Wilson prepare the way for peace and the League of Nations. But, as had happened in Schenectady, Lippman became disenchanted with politics, preferring the life of a critic than a practical problem solver, that lofty goal being seemingly unattainable due to the limitations of people. "The most incisive comment on politics today is indifference," he wrote. Lippman resigned soon after the war, returned to the U.S. and restarted his career in journalism. He gained enormous fame as a columnist and editor for the New York World, and when that paper was sold in 1931, Lippman became a syndicated columnist for the New York Herald-Tribune. He spent his career writing in New York, Washington, and New York again, and was awarded the Pulitzer Prize for his newspaper column in 1958 and 1962.

In June 1933, 21 years after he visited Lunn in Schenectady, Lippmann returned to the city to give the commencement speech at Union College's graduation ceremony. Lippmann mentioned his earlier time in Schenectady to open his talk, but then never went back to it again.

"It is amidst many rememberances that I return here today after an absence of 20 years," said Lippmann. "It was here in Schenectady, as a young man just out of college, that for four months I served my apprenticeship in practical politics and the practical administration of public affairs and where I first learned to distinguish between my theories and the facts, between my hopes and the realities of human affairs, and for that reason I am deeply grateful and to it I have tried to adhere."

Lippman's political and social evolution and his viewpoint on the human race and its limitations have long been the subject of college dissertations as well as column fodder for news-papermen who came after him. He often referred to himself as a 'liberal Democrat," a description that leaves many historians a bit befuddled. Instead, his lack of faith in the people and his support of capitalism long ago earned him the moniker of "former liberal."

In the 1960s, Lippmann got back into politics in an unof-ficial way, virtually earning a spot in President Johnson's inner circle during the fight for the Great Society; in particular civil rights legislation. He endorsed Johnson for reelection in 1964, but then broke with the president over Vietnam, considering it "supreme folly" to get involved in a land war in Asia. Lippmann wrote his final column, "Today and Tomorrow," on May 25, 1967, but continued being a contributor to Newsweek for four more years. He wrote his last magazine article in January 1971, and on December 14, 1974, nine months following the death of his wife, Helen, Lippmann died of a heart attack. He was 85.

CHAPTER 13

Where's Helen?

In his letter of resignation to Lunn, Lippman wrote of his hand-picked successor, John Macy, "I am sure you will find him an asset to the city, a power to your administration, and a delightful person to have as a friend."

A Detroit native, Macy was 12 years older than Lippmann. He grew up in the Boston area, and in 1895 headed to Harvard where he was an active and popular student, serving as the editor-in-chief of the school newspaper, The Harvard Advocate. Macy also worked on the staff of the Harvard Lampoon and served as class poet. He graduated from Harvard with honors (Phi Beta Kappa) in 1899, earned a master's the following year and began teaching in the school's English department. By the time he reached Schenectady, Macy was already an accomplished author and freelance journalist, but his major claim to fame was his association with Helen Keller. In 1902, Macy and Keller, who was blind, deaf and mute, collaborated on "The Story of My Life," a series in the Ladies' Home Journal that helped turned Keller into a national hero. A year later in 1903 the series was published in book form as Keller's autobiography and became a best-seller. A year later Keller graduated from Radcliffe, the first deaf and blind person to do so, and in 1905 Macy married Anne Sullivan, Keller's teacher, and the three lived together in Wrentham, a small town in Massachusetts about halfway between Boston and Providence, Rhode Island. On Wednesday, April 17, 1912, the Schenectady Gazette reported Lippman's exit and Macy's impending arrival. The article also trumpeted the prospect that along with Macy, his wife and Keller would also be coming to Schenectady. Since his time at Harvard, Macy showed an interest in politics, and by 1909 he had become an enthusiastic Socialist. He also fostered Keller's thoughts on socialism, and she soon was every bit as excited about the philosophy as Macy. Sullivan, meanwhile, remained aloof from politics.

While the news that Keller was coming to live in Schenectady created a great buzz in the city, the whole affair eventually became a big disappointment to Lunn and was probably embarrassing as well. On April 23 he had appointed the first woman to a city post when he put Mary Van Vorst, the wife of attorney James Van Vorst, on the new public welfare board. It was assumed that Lunn was going to also select Keller to serve on the board, but by the middle of June, with Macy having already been working in the city for seven weeks, Keller and Sullivan were still in Wrentham. On June 13, a New York Times' headline read "Schenectady Mayor Appoints Deaf and Dumb Author to Welfare Board," when in fact the two had never met or even officially corresponded with each other. On June 28, the newspapers learned that Keller wasn't coming until September, and on September 3 the Gazette reported that Keller was leaving Wrentham and coming to Schenectady. On September 5, however, an updated story said that Keller and Sullivan wouldn't be showing up until November.

"Miss Keller did make plans to come to this city early this fall, but she is now working on her voice and will not interrupt her study by leaving Wrentham until she has tried the experiment of giving public lectures," Macy told the Gazette. "This will be her first attempt to make public speeches, and she is busy making preparations. Her first lecture will be in November, so you can see she will not be here for at least two months.

"Miss Keller, however, is positively coming to Schenectady," said Macy assuredly. "Whether successful or not with her lectures, she will come to this city, and when she comes the mayor will appoint her to the Board of Public Welfare. He has not appointed her yet; he has not even written to her about it."

Macy then admonished the reporters gathered around him for their impatience.

"Most of the talk in the press about her duties and her services in New York has been premature. You newspapermen are so eager for her stories that you make things happen before they happen. The very first day that Miss Keller is here, I promise you that she will receive all the reporters. I will see to it personally that you are notified."

As it turned out, however, Keller's first public speech wasn't until February of 1913 in Montclair, N.J., and it didn't go well. "Terror invaded my flesh, my mind froze, my heart stopped beating," she wrote later of the experience. "I kept repeating, 'what shall I do? What shall I do to calm this tumult within me?'" Despite Sullivan's presence, Keller looked terrified, and at the conclusion of the Montclair event hurried off the stage in tears. She did, however, get better. By January of 1916 Keller was speaking out against U.S. involvement in World War I before a packed house at Carnegie Hall, and she would go on speaking in front of enthralled audiences for another half-century.

She never, however, came to Schenectady. On Sept. 21 it became official. Macy surprised Lunn with a written resignation and the next day returned to Wrentham. Keller and Sullivan, who was often dealing with poor health, would remain in Massachusetts. However, in a Nov. 3, 1912 article in the New York Call titled "How I Became a Socialist,", Keller explained why her Schenectady plans never materialized. She detailed the evolution of her political philosophy and attacked most of the newspapers in the Northeast for their coverage of her proposed move to Schenectady.

"I have never been in Schenectady," wrote Keller. "I have never met Mayor Lunn. I have never had a letter from him, but he has sent kind messages to me through Mr. Macy. Owing to Mrs. Macy's illness, whatever plans I had to join the workers in Schenectady have been abandoned."

Keller's article turned into a defense of Lunn and an indictment of the press, with the exception of a few socialist newspapers. Keller particularly disliked the headline in the Common Cause, a newspaper created in 1909 to support the women's suffrage movement. It read, "Schenectady Reds are Advertising; Using Helen Keller, the Blind Girl, to Receive Publicity." The article began, "it would be difficult to imagine anything more pathetic than the present exploitation of poor Helen Keller by the Socialists of Schenectady. For weeks the party's press agencies have heralded the fact that she is a Socialist, and is about to become a member of Schenectady's new Board of Public Welfare."

Keller, however, pointed out that nothing was printed in The Citizen about her coming to Schenectady, and that it was the Knickerbocker Press in Albany that broke the news. "It was telegraphed all over the country, and then began the real newspaper exploitation," wrote Keller. "By the socialist press? No, by the capitalist press. The Socialist papers printed the news, and some of them wrote editorials of welcome. But The Citizen, Mayor Lunn's paper, preserved silence and did not mention my name during all the weeks when the reporters were telephoning and telegraphing and asking for interviews. It was the capitalist press that did the exploiting."

The Common Cause had also printed that "Mr. and Mrs. Macy are enthusiastic Marxist propagandists, and it is scarcely surprising that Miss Keller, depending upon this lifelong friend for her most intimate knowledge of life, should have imbibed such opinions."

Keller's retort was clear. "Mr. Macy may be an enthusiastic Marxist propagandist, though I am sorry to say he has not shown much enthusiasm in propagating his Marxism through my fingers. Mrs. Macy is not a Marxist, nor a Socialist. Therefore, what the Common Cause says about her is not true. The editor must have invented that, made it out of whole cloth, and if that is the way his mind works, it is no wonder that he is opposed to socialism. He has not sufficient sense of fact to be a socialist or anything else intellectually worthwhile."

Along with her criticism of the Common Cause, Keller derided the work of the New York Times and the Brooklyn Eagle, writing that the Times had "bad ethics, bad logic and bad manners," and that the Eagle was "socially blind and deaf." Despite being harangued all summer by the press, Keller revealed that for the most part she did like newspapermen, and had no complaints about the socialist press. "No Socialist newspaper, neither the Call nor the National Socialist, ever asked me for an article. The editor of The Citizen hinted to Mr. Macy that he would like one, but he was too fine and considerate to ask for it point blank."

Also in the article, Keller said that she first became attracted to socialism after reading "New Worlds for Old" by H.G. Wells, on the recommendation of Mrs. Macy. A pamphlet, "New Worlds" was part of a series of articles Wells wrote between 1901-1908 about the future of socialism. At this time Wells was actively trying to reform the Fabian Society, a British organization created to advance the principles of socialism through gradual reform efforts, instead of more revolutionary tactics. But, while it may have been Sullivan who gave her the book, Keller reiterated her mentor wasn't a Socialist. "When she gave me the book, she was not a Socialist and she is not a Socialist now. Perhaps she will be one before Mr. Macy and I are done arguing with her."

As it turned out, it was Keller, following World War I, the Russian Revolution and a general disillusionment felt by many supporters of socialism, who left the party and set her sight on other causes, most particularly the American Association of the Blind. In the 1930s, however, Keller indicated to Eleanor Roosevelt that she still had some devotion to her lost cause. "Some of the things I said at the time are now out of date," she wrote in a letter to the First Lady, "but the spirit of revolt . . . remains."

Keller met President Grover Cleveland in 1887 when she was 7, and 12 presidents later in 1961 she was at the White House with John F. Kennedy. She died on June 1, 1968 at the age of 87.

As for Macy, Lunn was well familiar with him when his second secretary showed up in Schenectady to take over for Lippmann. "I very much regret losing Mr. Lippmann," Lunn told the Union-Star, "for he has been of inestimable service to me. But, now that he has to go, I am especially glad that his successor is to be his personal friend, and from my own knowledge of Mr. Macy, I am assured that he will be a distinct gain for the Administration."

Macy worked well with Lunn for much of 1912, but he, like Lippman, also found Schenectady's brand of socialism a bit wanting. He began writing a book after leaving Schenectady, and in 1916 "Socialism in America" sold pretty well. In it, Macy criticized Lunn and his administration for working within the capitalistic system. Lunn's failure to raise taxes and his inability to mold the school system in the socialist image ruined any chance of the Schenectady experiment from working according to Macy. Unlike Lippman, however, Macy never lost his socialist idealogy. "Socialism in America," alienated him from his alma mater and put an end to his membership in the Harvard Club of New York, but he remained a leftist the rest of his life, working for various newspapers and magazines.

Macy's reason for leaving Schenectady was due to the "continuing illness" of his wife, but in reality the marriage was difficult and strained. There were more separations and by 1914 the two would never live together again, although Sullivan refused to grant him a divorce. Macy fell in love with another woman in 1920, a deaf mute, and had a child with her. But the last decade of his life was a struggle marked by sadness. Alcoholism led to an overall decline in his health and in 1932, a few years after his companion died, Macy also passed away.

CHAPTER 14

A Long Hot Summer

At the New York State Socialist Convention in Auburn during the first week of July 1912, Lunn's name was not placed in nomination for any state-wide office, fueling speculation that the party had bigger plans for the Schenectady mayor. Obviously, according to several New York newspapers printed on July 2, it meant that Lunn would be the Socialist candidate for Congress in the fall.

Just when the thought first popped into his head is unclear. Perhaps it was a staunch supporter that initially verbalized the idea, but what is clear is that, despite some problems at home with his own party, Lunn was becoming a popular figure across the state, and a run for a seat in the U.S. House of Representatives suddenly seemed like a realistic possibility. People were discovering that Lunn was an extremely likable politician and a first-rate vote getter. It would be a long, hot summer however, and unless Lunn was being disingenuous, he didn't initially give the idea of a run for congress any serious deliberation.

Meanwhile, back on May 27, Schenectady's City Council was volatile as ever. Alderman William D. Dunn, a Republican from the First Ward, presented an anti-red flag resolution ensuring that the Stars and Stripes would never be usurped by the Socialist colors. Alderman M.A. Dancy, a Socialist from the Second Ward, moved that the resolution be sent "to the wastebasket," and fellow Socialist William Turnbull of the Sixth Ward argued that the resolution was "out of order and uncalled for." Ninth Ward Alderman Harvey A. Simmons, just back from the national Socialist convention in Indianapolis, called it the "performance of a clown," and Timothy W. Burns of the Thirteenth Ward, also a Socialist, said it was "an insult to the Socialists and the whole city of Schenectady." It was Noonan who came up with the most practical response, suggesting that the resolution "lay on the table until Alderman Dunn could bring evidence to substantiate his charge that the Socialists intended to supplant the red, white and blue with the red." Noonan's suggestion was passed unanimously, even Alderman Dunn concurring with the motion.

Lunn didn't weigh in on the flag controversy but he had plenty of other issues occupying his time. When Duane Avenue grocer Max Stern died in early June, a group of Hungarian Jews sought an injunction from the courts to prevent Stern from being buried in Vale Cemetery. Instead, they wanted him interred in a Jewish cemetery in the Carman neighborhood in the southeastern section of the city. Stern was a Jew, but evidently not a serious practitioner of his faith, and his wife was a Catholic. Stern was also a devout Socialist, and the treasurer of the English chapter of the local party. He had suddenly dropped dead in Karl Marx Hall in the Mont Pleasant section of the city, and most of his Socialist friends, in solidarity with his wife, wanted him buried in Vale. The injunction wasn't granted, Stern was finally buried at Vale, and conducting the funeral service was the mayor of the city, selected as a "compromise pastor" by the Catholics and the Jews.

That same week, Lunn was at the mayors' conference in Utica talking about the immorality of segregation, and when he returned it was back to work overseeing municipal ventures into the ice, coal and produce business, all with varying degrees of success. Lunn came to believe it was impossible to create a local socialist society in the city, preferring instead to strive for the "betterment of local conditions for the mass of the people." However, he would apply socialist principles when he could, and in the first half of 1912 that meant not only coal, ice and groceries from the city, but also a municipal farm, a Department of Maternity and Infancy Nursing, an employment bureau and free lodging for homeless men.

Lunn indeed had a lot on his plate heading into the summer of 1912, and the prospect of running for Congress and taking on new responsibilities and formulating new goals, with so much of the fight at home in Schenectady barely begun, had to be a bit daunting.

Lunn began the state convention in Auburn fighting against the notion that churches should be taxed. Despite his reasoning and the arguments of a few others, the motion was voted on, passed and added to the state plank. In other business, Lunn was defeated in an attempt to become chairman of the state party, losing to Gustav Strebel of Syracuse. He was, however, elected vice-chairman for the state group.

Along with Lunn as a possible candidate for Congress, Simmons, Schenectady's Ninth Ward assemblyman, was also in the running. In fact, according to the Gazette on July 2, "That the Socialist candidate for Congress from this district will be selected from this city is a certainty." The Gazette also reported that "Mayor Lunn has stated he is not a candidate for the position, and Alderman Simmons told a Gazette reporter yesterday afternoon that he would accept the nomination if the members of the Socialist Party wanted him to run."

Lunn had left Auburn and returned to Schenectady to deal with other matters, such as how the city should best celebrate the Fourth of July. As they had been for years, fireworks were a major part of July 4th celebrations in 1912. The year before, however, celebrations around the country were marked by tragedies caused directly by fireworks, and Lunn felt the time was right for Schenectady to enjoy a more calm and peaceful holiday. On Wednesday July 3, Lunn issued a proclamation forbidding the use of fireworks, calling for the people to celebrate in a "safe and sane" way. Lunn had plenty of statistical evidence to support his claim that fireworks were dangerous. He wrote that "during the past eight years 33,885 people have been killed or wounded as a result of Fourth of July celebrations." In July 1911, an entire town in Pennsylvania was nearly wiped out due to a fire started by a Roman candle on the Fourth, while Pittsburgh reported three deaths and 45 injuries and Philadelphia nearly 400 injured in fireworks celebrations. In Chicago on that same day in 1911, firemen responded to a record 164 alarms, almost all of them fireworks related. In place of fireworks, Lunn and the city would offer free ice cream, band concerts, "an aeroplane demonstration and the most elaborate electrical water display ever given the city on the river at night."

Along with how best to celebrate the Fourth, Lunn, as well as the entire Northeast, was dealing with what would become a long heat wave and eventually lead to drought-like conditions that threatened the city's access to fresh milk. On June 24, when things were just starting to heat up, a young boy drowned while swimming in the Erie Canal just west of the city. On July 8, with temperatures in the high 90s and officials hoping to avoid any reoccurrence of such accidents, Schenectady police stuck to the letter of the law and arrested four teenage boys for swimming in the canal. The heat heightened another major issue of that summer when on July 3, Lunn and the Socialist administration were hit with an injunction prohibiting the city from selling ice. David V. Maxwell, a grocer and ice dealer whose store was located at 714 Crane Street, said that the sale of ice by the city was "for the purpose of advertising the Socialist administration," and that its sale was "wholly unauthorized by the second-class cities law." Maxwell's lawyer, Del B. Salmon, presented his case to State Supreme Court Justice William Rudd of Albany, who slapped the injunction on the city's ice business, restraining Mayor Lunn, City Comptroller John L. Myers, City Treasurer Phillip Andres, Commissioner of Public Works Charles A. Mullen and Superintendent of Water Fred W. Bentley from participating in the ice business.

The papers were served around 1:30 p.m. that Wednesday afternoon of July 3, which according to a Gazette headline the next day resulted in the mayor and his staff being "Thrown into Furor." The five men in city wagons that had been delivering ice since May 15 were immediately called to the mayor's office. Although Morris Hillquist, the city's legal counsel, was not in the city at the time, Lunn and his cohorts huddled for more than an hour to determine what course of action they would take. What they came up with was George R. Lunn and Associates.

Lunn argued that since the city sold water, it was legal to sell ice. He apparently understood, however, that selling ice and selling water, even though they were both $H2O$, was not necessarily a winning argument legally. When approached by reporters early that Tuesday evening, Lunn had a statement ready.

"The City of Schenectady, the mayor, the commissioner of public works, the superintendent of water, and other city officials have all been restrained from selling ice to the people of Schenectady. An injunction has been issued tying the city's hands and absolutely prohibiting it from serving the customers, of which the city already has 1,000. This injunction came as a bolt from a clear sky, without warning, and was calculated to have the city drop its 1,000 customers and leave them in the lurch without ice in the first warm days of July."

Lunn went on to say that the city would obey the court's ruling and that the water bureau and the city would sell no more ice. However, Lunn argued that the administration was made up of individual citizens, and that a new business venture named George R. Lunn and Associates would sell ice to city residents.

"But the people will not be left without ice," continued Lunn. "The city will not sell ice, but ice will be sold at 25 cents a hundred pounds, at that. The city officials enjoined as city officials are free individuals. All who wish ice can have it tomorrow and ever after at 25 cents per hundred pounds from George R. Lunn and Associates. Men and teams will be employed, ice bought at wholesale and sold at retail, and the people who have had confidence in the present city administration will find that their elective officials are ready officially, or if that is prohibited, personally to fill their pledges."

The city's municipal ice house, located at the end of Ingersoll Avenue near the Mohawk River, had started operation earlier that year on January 26 when Lunn hired 25 men to cut "ice cakes" from the river. The job lasted about two weeks, and by July there was still plenty of ice – nearly 2,000 tons – available for Schenectady residents to last into the fall. That next morning the same city workers, now acting as employees of George R. Lunn & Associates, headed out in their wagons delivering ice despite concerns that they might be held in contempt of court, the injuction stating that "city officials should not directly or indirectly sell ice."

At this point Lunn and his associates thought it best to sell the ice at auction, although there was concern that this decision too might be interpreted as contempt of court. The plan was for a representative of Lunn to buy the ice from the city, and while Maxwell had hoped to outbid the mayor and purchase the ice himself, Lunn's representative, one Daniel J. Sweeney, prevailed. According to the July 16 Gazette, Sweeney paid $175 for more than 1,000 tons of ice, keeping George R. Lunn & Associates in business. Maxwell's lawyer kept hammering away at the administration, suggesting that city property was being used illegally and asking, "why the ice company should not be prohibited from weighing the ice on city scales."

It was a busy summer for City Corporation Counsel Frank Cooper. Not only was he dealing with the ice issue, but on July 26 Maxwell and Salmon combined forces again to impose an injuction on the city's municipal grocery store. There was more. Later that year Lunn and Associates also entered into the coal business. The legal fight over these municipal enterprises lasted into 1913, with the ice and grocery ventures evolving into cooperative enterprises before being eliminated by the new administration after Lunn lost the 1913 election. As for coal, George R. Lunn and Associates worked well for a while according to George MacAdam's summary of Schenectady's Socialist administration, printed in the New York Times in November of 1917.

"The first snag encountered was when the only wholesale coal dealer in Schenectady refused to sell to George R. Lunn and Associates on the grounds that, since they were avowedly out to undersell, the regular retail distributors would naturally object.

"But the city had a contract with the obstinate wholesaler for the purchase of coal at 20 cents per ton more than the retailers were paying," wrote MacAdam. "So, the association took the coal bought under city contract, retailed it to the public at 50 cents per ton less than the market rate, collected cash, and reimbursed the city as each ton was sold. The Associates were not, however, losing as much money by this deal as it would appear, for the city bought coal from itself for its public buildings, and the profit made here was used to wipeout the other deficit."

In her book, "The Rise of the Public Authority: State Building and Economic Development in Twentieth Century America," Gail Radford wrote that Lunn's coal business "may well have been successful in commercial terms and in any case put competitive pressure on private firms to hold down their rates during the two winter months the Lunn administration was in office."

Lunn, did in fact, remain in the coal business after his first term in the mayor's office was over. According to city directories of that time, he was listed as a coal dealer with a business address at 116 South Centre Street up until 1919. As for ice, New York State Supreme Court Justice H.T. Kellogg put an end to that on August 5, 1913, when he ruled that the mayor, comptroller, treasurer, commissioner of public works and superintendent of the water department or anyone serving as their agents are permanently barred from carrying on any kind of business dealing with ice.

In his order, Kellogg wrote: "That plaintiff [Maxwell] is entitled to judgment forever restraining and enjoining the above-named defendant officers and each of them and their deputies, agents, attorneys, employees and servants from directly or indirectly or in any manner, selling or exposing ice and ice tickets for sale and from soliciting customers for said ice and said ice tickets."

George Lunn posed for this photograph sometime around 1910, after he left as pastor of the First Reformed Church and before he was elected mayor of Schenectady.

George Lunn was around 30 years old when this photo was taken, probably just before he came to Schenectady in 1904 to become pastor of the First Reformed Church.

George Lunn, standing farthest to the right on the platform, posed for this picture while serving as editor of The Citizen during the summer of 1911, before announcing he would run for mayor as a Socialist.

This photograph of Lunn shows him busy at work in the mayor's office at the City Hall Annex in 1912.

"THE ROOSEVELT STORY" Produced by TOLA PRODUCTIONS, Inc.
Permission is hereby granted for reproduction by newspapers, magazines, trade publications and exhibitors' displays — Made in U. S. A.

George Lunn, left, was lieutenant governor under New York Gov. Al Smith, right, when the pair met with two other powerful Democrats, Franklin Delano Roosevelt, second from left, and West Virginia's John W. Davis, in August of 1924 at FDR's home in Hyde Park. Davis was the Democratic candidate for president that November, losing to incumbent Calvin Coolidge.

On October 10, 1931, George Lunn, having recently been named Commander of the United Spanish War Veterans, visited the White House where he was met by President Herbert Hoover and Gen. Frank Hines of the Veterans Bureau. *Image courtsey of ACME Newspictures*

The Citizen, the newspaper Lunn created back in 1910, took aim at their former editor with this political cartoon from 1918 after Lunn had officially become a Democrat.

CHAPTER 15

The Campaign for Congress

While David Maxwell and his lawyer argued with the Socialist Local over ice, groceries, and coal, Lunn suddenly found himself in a hospital bed. On July 16, while driving around Schenectady with Mullen in the city automobile, Lunn began feeling ill and was taken to his home on Jay Street. After resting, the mayor began feeling better and attended the theater that night with his wife. But by 7 a.m., the next morning, Dr. Faust, having been summoned, diagnosed the condition as an appendicitis attack and ordered a quick visit to Ellis Hospital. By 9 a.m., Lunn's pain was significantly worse and by 11 he was on the operating table with Faust performing the surgery. The mayor came through the operation fine and Faust and his attendant physicians all reported, according to the Gazette, that "there is practically no doubt of his rapid recovery."

Although the health crisis had passed, Lunn needed time to convalesce, and recovering from surgery in 1912 wasn't a speedy process. His hospital stay after the operation was two weeks, and then for most of the summer he was recuperating either at home or George Foster Peabody's summer residence on Lake George. City Council President Russell Hunt ended up serving as acting mayor until Lunn finally returned to office the first week of September. During the nearly two-month absence from office, Lunn had plenty of time to contemplate running for Congress.

Soon after returning from the state convention in Auburn, Lunn was selected by his fellow Socialists in Schenectady as their preferred candidate for the 30th Congressional district. At a meeting of the Schenectady local at the Red Men's Hall on Saturday night, July 6, Lunn defeated Simmons by a vote of 120-97. When asked by a member if he would accept the nomination, Lunn made no reply, and when someone suggested that the mayor's name be stricken from the list of candidates, Lunn seconded the motion. The motion, however, was voted down by the rest of the membership.

The meeting, presided over by Lunn's assistant pastor at the United People's Church, the Rev. Robert Bakeman, went from 8 p.m., to midnight. Near the end of the night, Lunn was cornered by reporters and asked for a comment on his candidacy.

"I appreciate the endorsement of the Socialists from Schenectady County," said Lunn. "Whether I shall accept the nomination for Congress is a matter for future decision."

In Monday's newspaper, The Gazette suggested that some of those hoping to send Lunn to Congress were doing so because they wanted him out of the city and were hoping to put Russell Hunt in the mayor's office. Another group genuinely supported the idea of Lunn heading to Congress, as did Socialists at the national level, such as presidential candidate Eugene Debs, his running mate, Emil Seidel of Milwaukee, Wisconsin Congressman Victor Berger, and Lunn's legal advisor in New York City, Morris Hillquist. The Gazette also offered the opinion that while the Schenectady Socialists may control the party in the 30th district, those thinking Lunn could win a seat in Congress were unacquainted with the overall political picture of the region.

Lunn's appendicitis attack and his recovery conveniently put him out of the spotlight for the final two weeks of July and all of August. When Corporation Counsel Frank Cooper and his wife returned from a visit with the Lunns in Westport on Lake Champlain on August 20, the possibility of the mayor making a run for Congress seemed remote. After spending a week with Lunn, Cooper said the mayor "is not strongly inclined to run for Congress, but that considerable influence has been brought to bear upon the mayor to accept the nomination." Cooper led reporters to believe that "Lunn's health is not very good and that it will not permit him to make a very strenuous campaign," stated the article. Cooper also suggested that Lunn "is of the opinion that he ought to carry out the administration of mayor rather than accept a nomination, which might offer him a seat in Congress." Cooper's final piece of information from his trip to Westport was that Lunn expected to return to work in Schenectady soon, and nearly two weeks later, on Tuesday, Sept. 3, Lunn was back at his desk in the City Hall Annex.

"I am feeling fine," said Lunn, who left Lake Champlain on Saturday and spent Sunday and Monday at the Knower House in Altamont, a summer home he rented just 15 miles southwest of Schenectady, "I had the best of treatment at Ellis Hospital, and when I knew what it was that had me I couldn't get to the operating table quick enough."

According to both Schenectady newspapers, Lunn seemed as robust as ever, and within two days of his return, his thoughts on running for Congress became clear. Mr. Paul H. Doty, Chairman of the Socialist Congressional Committee from the 30th District in Amsterdam, received a letter from Lunn dated September 5 stating he could not accept the party's nomination to run for Congress.

"I appreciate more deeply than I can express the honor which the Socialists of the thirtieth congressional district have conferred upon me in designating me as their nominee for Congress," Lunn wrote. "The privilege of representing the cause of Socialism as an official within the halls of Congress is an opportunity for immense service."

Lunn went on to say: "At this particular period in our political history it would give me special satisfaction to be present in Congress to oppose in every way possible the continuance of a system that grinds the life out of millions of our men and women and no less than 2,000,000 of our helpless child workers. I am speaking thus for I confidently believe that my nomination in the thirtieth district would lead to election.

"After more careful thought, however, covering the several weeks of my absence from the city, I have come to the conclusion that while my pleasure would be to run for Congress, my duty demands that I remain in my present position to which I have been elected by the people of this city. In declining the nomination, I do so with the desire that whatever powers in the way of campaigning I may have may be used to elect some other comrade as a representative of the army of workers of this district.

"My plain duty," summed up Lunn, "to the people of Schenectady and the Socialist Party is to continue my work as mayor."

Simmons seemed to be everyone's second choice, and according to a Union-Star story he had badly wanted to be his party's congressional nominee. But after silently fuming and waiting all summer for Lunn to make up his mind, by the first week in September Simmons was adamant about not accepting a run for Congress. Daniel J. Sweeney, a cigar maker with a shop on Jay Street in downtown Schenectady, had his name thrown around as a possible candidate, as did Common Council President Hunt and Seventh Ward alderman Noonan. Both battle-scarred veterans in politics, Hunt or Noonan might have gathered up enough momentum to secure a nomination, but there were other members of the Socialist local who felt that if Lunn wasn't going to run, the honor should go to some other party leader from outside Schenectady County. There were also rumblings, according to the Gazette, that Lunn's comrades would not allow him to refuse the nomination.

The next meeting of the Schenectady local, on Tuesday night, September 10, was filled with friction. A Gazette headline blared, "Meeting of Socialist Local Marked by Bitter Personalities and Accusations." Another headline read, "Lack of Harmony in Organization Admitted," but in the largest type was the news that said, "Compel Mayor to Run for Congress."

Simmons decried the vicious in-fighting in the organization, and although he suggested Lunn would be the best man to "bring about harmony in the ranks of the party," he also conceded that the mayor was right in wanting to remain in Schenectady and do the work he was designated to do. State Assemblyman Herbert Merrill argued that Lunn should not be allowed to refuse the nomination, according to the Gazette, reporting that "his resignation appeared to have cast discredit on the members of the local party in that it would appear that there were none here who could carry on the city government."

Noonan, meanwhile, red-faced according to the Gazette, rose to argue against Simmons' contentions, shouting across the floor, "I say it would be a reflection on Dr. Lunn if we did not insist on his running for the office." Simmons responded by saying what many may have been thinking, "I make this statement right here on the floor of this meeting, that they want to get rid of Dr. Lunn," his words resulting in a brief but awkward silence. Alderman Burns got things riled up again with an attack on Simmons, and finally, after some more heated exchanges and the meeting bordering on "chaos," according to Simmons, Lunn took the floor.

The Gazette article, paraphrasing Lunn's words, reported that the mayor concluded by saying "that if the local thought he should carry out his term as mayor he would do it, and if they wanted him to run he would." Merrill then read a letter from the state's attorney general regarding primary law, stating that it was too late for Lunn to withdraw, and around midnight a vote was finally taken, keeping Lunn as the party's candidate for Congress.

On Sept. 19, a Saturday night, Lunn officially launched his campaign for Congress with a speech at Crescent Park. There were nearly 6,000 people there according to The Citizen's account, which wasn't published until the following Friday, the paper still being a weekly. Both the Gazette and the Union-Star, which did not publish on Sunday, failed to mention the event in their Monday editions. They did, however, take the opportunity to tell their readers about every note of disharmony coming out of the Socialist local, and there certainly was plenty. While most successful and popular politicians, like Lunn, would have been riding a wave of euphoria as they planned a campaign for Congress, the Mayor of Schenectady in the late summer of 1912 had enough distractions to keep any rampant enthusiasm in check.

In late July, Hawley Van Vechten, the county clerk and Lunn's right-hand man at The Citizen, was reported to be throwing his support behind Simmons' bid for Congress, which according to the Union-Star, irritated Lunn backers to the point where they decided to demand his resignation. His replacement had already been selected according to the newspaper, which in the same article reported that "Lunn Socialists laugh at the whole story. One of the most prominent Socialists in town," continued the article, "while admitting there is much ill-feeling and recrimination over the congressional nomination, and saying that it is probably some young Socialists who were not as careful as they might have been, declared there was nothing in the report about forcing Mr. Van Vechten out. He has made an efficient city clerk, said the man, who is high in the councils of the party, and he was emphatic in saying he knew nothing about any intention to spring the city clerk's resignation upon him."

Van Vechten, always an independent thinker, "has got into line again with the Lunn Socialists," the Union-Star reported on August 2. How he felt about the newspaper's characterization of his feelings is unknown, and while Van Vechten did apparently change his support from Simmons to Lunn, "he tried to treat the whole matter of a growing demand for his resignation from office as a joke," wrote the Union-Star. The article did quote Van Vechten as saying Mayor Lunn is the only Socialist, "who would have even a fighting chance to win the congressional berth." He also said, "I'm not losing any sleep over my job."

Although the problem of Van Vechten's reputed defection was no longer an issue, on September 23, four days after Lunn made his bid for Congress official, Ben Henry, Lunn's business manager at The Citizen, announced his resignation from the job as well as his complete repudiation of socialism. Henry was given ample space by both Schenectady newspapers to explain his decision and opine about the failings and weaknesses of socialism, calling it "delusional." Only a few days earlier, Macy had handed in his resignation as had Morris Hillquist, Lunn's special counsel who was seriously ill. Of course, according to Schenectady's two newspapers, Lunn support was quickly evaporating in his own camp, pointing out also the resignation of Bakeman as assistant pastor at the United People's Church and Lippman's exit way back in the spring.

Henry's long, rambling statement to the press didn't include a lot of specific details as to why he was so disappointed in socialism, but it did point out the obvious human foibles that threaten any such rigid political group.

"The longer I stayed the more disgusted I became with the delusion and inconsistency of socialism as I beheld it," he said. "I resolved to follow my conscience and get out of this deluded rut and to do so at once, lest I might get so filled up with dope and become like an opium fiend, unable to leave its dreamy atmosphere of self-hypnotism, making one's self believe the impossible and impractical. Not unlike the opium fiend raving for dope are some of the wild clamoring, abusive language, wholesale denouncement of everything except what they want, and they are willing in some cases to sacrifice all to get it."

As if not to offend any particular member of the group, Henry added that "personally, as individuals I am on the best of terms with everybody in the party and everyone connected to the newspaper."

In the September 27 edition of The Citizen, Charles W. Wood summed up Henry's action, suggesting he was a nice man but never really a Socialist. "He just drifted into membership in the Socialist Party as some children drift into a Sunday school," said Wood. He was nothing more than "a nominal member of the party."

Things got better for Lunn the first week in October when Eugene Debs, the Socialist presidential candidate, visited Schenectady on a Sunday night and spoke before a standing room only audience at Proctor's Theater alongside the Erie Canal. The Citizen reported that 2,100 people paid 25 cents apiece to listen to Debs, and nearly that same number were turned away. Again, while the Gazette and Union Star, in the days leading up to Debs' appearance, questioned the morality of charging 25 cents ahead on a Sunday night to listen to a political speech, they had nothing to say about his address in the next day's paper. The Citizen, however, provided plenty of coverage.

"Never once did the grand old warrior stoop to political trickery during the speech," said The Citizen. "He just reached out with all his soul to the souls of the workers, asking them for nothing, promising them nothing but inspiring them in every cadence with the realization that there was no limit to what they might accomplish for themselves."

The Citizen printed nearly the entirety of Debs' speech, including a reference to Lunn's introduction.

"As Dr. Lunn said – and rightly – this is something more than a political meeting. There is something more than political sentiment here. Standing in this overmastering presence, I am sure I can fearlessly preach the social revolution which is to sweep capitalism out of existence and usher in the new republic of socialism."

"We live in perhaps the most prosperous nation in the world," continued Debs. "We have the most marvelous production machinery on Earth. We have the millions of eager workers. We are ready to produce in abundance. Then why should the mass of our people be in poverty?... Let him that is greatest among you be the servant of all." After Debs' departure from Schenectady on Sunday night, Lunn said his message "was the best sermon that has been preached in Schenectady today."

A few days after Debs' visit, Lippman suddenly materialized in Schenectady and paid a surprise call on Lunn, offering his support. While his trip into the Maine woods was over, his move to the center politically had evidently not taken hold just yet. Although he would shun Debs and vote for Roosevelt the following month, in October Lippman still was obviously a big Lunn supporter regardless of the Socialist affiliation. Within the next five months, however, with the publication of "A Preface to Politics" in March of 1913, he would denounce socialism and progressivism.

"I came to Schenectady today to offer Mayor Lunn my services in the congressional campaign," Lippman told reporters. "It is a great pleasure to be able to do this because it is always more gratifying to be able to agree with a man than to disagree with him. On the subject of his election to Congress, no two Socialists can hold different opinions. All Dr. Lunn's splendid abilities will find their best use in the House of Representatives.

He can speak there not only for this district, but for the nation. The people of this community can make no better gift to the country than to elect him."

Lippman's busy schedule, he said, kept him from making too big a contribution to Lunn's bid.

"I wish my work were such that I could spend a few weeks in Schenectady in the campaign," he said. "That is impossible. But whatever I can do to help, I shall."

Joining Lunn as a candidate for the 63rd U.S. Congress were two businessmen and a college professor. Samuel Wallin, a former mayor of Amsterdam and an executive in the carpet industry, had won the Republican primary on Sept. 17 after incumbent Congressman, Henry Schermerhorn Deforest, decided not to run for re-election. DeForest had been the mayor of Schenectady back in 1885-87 and 1889-91. The Democratic candidate was another Amsterdamian, Robert E. Lee Reynolds, editor of the Amsterdam Daily Democrat and Recorder, and rounding out the field on the Progressive ticket was Union College professor Edward Everett Hale Jr., the head of the school's English department and the son of Edward Everett Hale, a Unitarian minister and author of the novel, "The Man Without a Country."

The campaign season, much shorter in those days, was shaping up to be great theater, but the race for Congress would be overshadowed by events taking place in a small textile town just west of the 30th district.

CHAPTER 16

Little Falls

Union problems played a big part in bringing Thomas Edison and his Edison Electrical Works to Schenectady in 1886, and the history of the General Electric Company is replete with strikes and other labor issues, including the famous sit-down strike in December of 1906. In August of 1912, however, GE President Charles A. Coffin, the man who surprised everyone by calling Lunn "the best man" for the mayoral job, and said he was going to work with him "hand and glove," was evidently feeling somewhat charitable. On Aug. 28, GE officials announced that the company would be offering a pension plan to its employees that would cost the company between $500,000 and $1 million. Men who reached 70 years of age and who had been at the company for 20 years would become eligible for a pension, as would women 60 years of age with 20 years of employment. Also, men of 65 and women of 55 who were incapacitated and could no longer work and had been at GE for 20 years would also become eligible for the pension.

For the 15,000 male and female employees working at the Schenectady plant during the summer of 1912 it was good news. Also, a senior official pointed out, the new pension plan would not benefit those high-level employees with high salaries as much as it would the average worker. While things were relatively harmonious at GE, labor relations were quite volatile for ALCO employees as well as other unskilled workers in Schenectady. And in Little Falls, a small city 60 miles to the west of Schenectady, conditions were even worse. For Helen Schloss, a Russian-born Jewish nurse and Socialist who was invited to Little Falls by some of the city's most prominent women, the workplace and lifestyle for an unskilled, immigrant worker, particularly female, was intolerable.

Schloss, who had worked for the New York City Public Board of Health, arrived in Little Falls in April of 1912 to help the city's social elite do its part in the statewide campaign to eradicate tuberculosis. Recruited to Little Falls by the Fortnightly Club, a group of women that included the wife of J. Judson Gilbert, owner of one of the largest textile mills in the city, Schloss was deeply troubled by the plight of the lower class there. On August 12 of that year she described those conditions to the Factory Investigating Commission, a group formed after the previous year's Triangle Shirtwaist Factory fire in New York City. With Schloss's testimony as well as its own fact-finding tour around upstate New York, the FIC came out with a blistering report in January of 1913. After investigating 419 factories in Central New York, the commission concluded that only 3.8 percent of the major employers offered separate lunch rooms for its workers, and in the "majority of the shops lunch is eaten at the machines, frequently with unwashed hands." Also, even in areas where there were poisonous substances, a separate lunch room "was still the exception to the rule."

Nowhere in the state were things as bad as they were in Little Falls, where one major employer, who was also a member of the local health board, couldn't be bothered to provide a bathroom for his workers. "The only toilet accommodation in the factory," said the FIC report, "is a barrel located in the cellar which is used as a water closet." While tuberculosis may have been a serious problem, Schloss discovered quickly that the poor working class in Little Falls had a mountain of trials and tribulations to deal with each and every day.

Little Falls had only been chartered as a city in 1895, and in 1910 there were around 10,000 people living there, many of them workers in the textile mills. While not on the same scale as Schenectady's, Little Falls did have its own marked population increase, with new Polish, Slavic, Ukrainian, Hungarian and Italian immigrants bringing the population total to over 12,000 by 1912. The two major employers were the Phoenix Knitting Mill and the Gilbert Knitting Mill, and many of the employees were women and children. Earlier that year, the New York State Legislature had passed a bill outlawing a 60-hour work week for these women and their children, and on October 1, the law went into effect. The mill owners, who had previously worked together to keep the hourly wage low, reluctantly went along with the bill but also reduced the pay rate, infuriating their female employees. On Wednesday, October 9, 80 workers from the Phoenix Mill walked off the job and on Monday, October 14, 76 from the Gilbert Mill joined them on the picket line. Within the next few days there were nearly 700 people on strike, more than two-thirds of them women, and by October 25, when the strikers had voted to affiliate with the Industrial Workers of the World, some accounts have the number at over 1,500.

While not as big as the strike earlier in the year in Lawrence, Mass., or as violent as the work stoppage in Paterson, New Jersey in 1913, the Little Falls Textile Strike of 1912 was a high profile event. Lunn's regular visits to Little Falls and his subsequent two arrests kept things on the front page, and all of the IWW's most well-known figures, such as Big Bill Haywood, Benjamin LeGere and Filippo Bocchini, were there. But along with the contributions of those prominent men in the labor struggle, Little Falls is also remembered and noteworthy for the work done by women, in particular Schloss and Matilda Robbins.

Schloss was born in Vilna, Russia in 1885, and 10 years later emigrated to America with her family. She learned English quickly, was an excellent student and soon became interested in socialism. In 1906, she was arrested after a demonstration in New York's theater district with a group of Harlem Socialist Club members, including Elizabeth Gurley Flynn. Flynn, who became one of the labor movements most celebrated figures, was just 15 at the time.

That same year, Schloss graduated from the School of Nursing at Bellevue Hospital and went to work for the NYC Board of Health. She also attended the Rand School of Social Science, a group started by Socialists, and held nursing positions with city health boards in Binghamton and Malone before returning to New York City. She was back home again, but only for a short time, before the fine ladies of Little Falls called.

Robbins, meanwhile, born Matilda Rabinowitz in the Ukraine in 1887, was two years younger than Schloss. She came to the U.S. with her family as a young girl, moving from New York City to Connecticut, and by the time she was 16 was supporting herself, working in a variety of factory jobs as well as nursing and childcare positions. She joined the Socialist Party in Bridgeport, Connecticut, and soon after the IWW. In 1912 she left her job and headed to Lawrence, Massachusetts, playing a minor role in the IWW effort there to organize that strike. Later that year in Little Falls, when IWW leaders Legere and Bocchini were jailed, Robbins again left Bridgeport in early November and headed to the central New York trouble where, at the age of 25, she basically ran the show. But a lot happened before Matilda's arrival on the scene.

Before the 80 workers, mostly female, began the strike on October 9, Schloss had been writing to fellow Socialists around the state asking for help, and she knew she had a sympathetic ear in Lunn. As a result, the Socialist local in Schenectady was ready. With the mayor's hearty endorsement, the Schenectady Socialists sent a small group, led by Rev. Bakeman, to Little Falls on Sunday afternoon, October 13. By Monday afternoon, Bakeman was in the Little Falls jail - his first of five arrests – and had telegraphed Lunn for assistance. Mullen and Philip Callery, Lunn's new secretary who had only been on the job for a couple of weeks, took the next train to Little Falls and arrived Monday evening around 7:30 p.m. Bakeman told them his story, how he had asked Chief of Police Dusty Long if he could speak and how Long had said yes, suggesting Clinton Park instead of a busy street corner. Bakeman did exactly what he was told, but at some point Chief Long evidently changed his mind, showed up at Clinton Park and arrested Bakeman.

The retired pastor turned rabid Socialist was arraigned later in the day and released on bail with a trial set for Wednesday morning, October 16.

While Callery stayed in Little Falls Monday night, Mullen took a late train back to Schenectady, arriving home after midnight. Tuesday morning, he was at Lunn's office early when the mayor got in, and after relating Bakeman's story, Mullen and Lunn got on the next train heading west and arrived in Little Falls that Tuesday around noon. A rally had been planned by the strikers at the train station for 12:30 p.m., and a small crowd had already formed when the mayor's train arrived. Mullen, whose account to Lunn indicated that the strikers now numbered 700, told the mayor to remain in the station while he found Bakeman and assessed the situation. On a signal from Mullen, Lunn walked out of the station and mounted a nearby bench and addressed the crowd.

"Citizens of Little Falls, I understand you have a strike on here," said Lunn, as the crowd, increasing in number, gathered closer to hear. "I am glad we live in a free country where we have the right to strike, and that we can publicly meet and state our grievances."

Not too long after Lunn got started a police officer approached and told him he could not speak. Lunn asked where he could speak, and soon Chief Long arrived on the scene and also told Lunn he could not address the strikers. According to Mullen's account, Long told Lunn to follow him, to which Lunn replied, "not unless I'm under arrest." The chief, who at this time did not know the identity of the troublemaker, informed the mayor that he was indeed under arrest, and grabbed Lunn by the lapel and escorted him to the Little Falls jail. Another officer had already grabbed Bakeman, arrest No. 2 for him, and Mullen, after pleading for an explanation of the charges, was also thrown into the jail although he was apparently released and allowed to act as the mayor's attorney,

After spending about three hours behind bars, Lunn and his group were released on their own recognizance by Judge Daniel Collins and a trial date was set for the following day, a Wednesday. By this time, attorney James J. Barry of Schenectady was in the courtroom representing Lunn, who nonetheless took charge of his defense. He cross-examined Chief Long, asking him if he had ever previously interrupted a public speaker for violating city ordinance's about "disturbing the peace" and "blocking traffic." Long replied that he had not, but that those speakers had obtained permits. Lunn then asked Long if he had arrested him for speaking without a permit, and Long responded that he was just following orders from the mayor, Frank Shall, whom Long felt had the right to determine who would and who would not be given a permit to speak. By the end of the day, Judge Collins had heard enough and announced that the case was being adjourned until November 1. He earlier denied Barry's motion to dismiss the charges against Lunn on the grounds that the city ordinance making possible the arrest was unconstitutional. Lunn informed the judge that he would continue to speak, and on the next day, Thursday, October 17, he was arrested again in Clinton Park.

On this day, a large crowd at Clinton Park was waiting for Lunn, whose inner circle included his wife, Mabel, Bakeman, Simmons, and Schenectady IWW organizer Rona G. DeGuerre. Lunn talked about Abraham Lincoln, again paraphrasing his words about people in this country "having the right to strike," and in due time Chief Long again interrupted the proceedings, arrested Lunn and took him to the Little Falls jail.

"We have a strike on our hands," Long told the press in a written statement, "and a foreign element to deal with. We have in the past kept them in subjection and we mean to continue to hold them – where they belong."

Lunn seemed ready and prepared to go to jail again, but the sight of his wife being escorted by police officers was a bit disconcerting. Looking back over his shoulder at his wife, Lunn reportedly yelled at Sheriff James Moon, "That's enough. Let Mrs. Lunn go." Reassured by Barry that no harm would befall his wife, Lunn relaxed and allowed Long to escort him to the police station.

But while Long and Moon may have felt fine about putting Lunn behind bars again, they weren't so sure about Mrs. Lunn. While her husband was talking in one section of Clinton Park, Mabel was in another area close by, reading a New York World editiorial about the unjust actions of policemen. While her husband and Henry L. Slobodin, state chairman of the Socialist Party, both threatened to "keep on pouring Socialist orators into Little Falls until the jails are full," the mayor's wife, a member of a prosperous New York City family, was not supposed to be part of the bargain.

Mrs. Lunn was never put in jail, but according to her account, printed in the Albany Times Union on Friday, October 18, there was no question in her mind she was under arrest.

"At my husband's request I had started to read an editorial from a New York newspaper when the sheriff caught me by the arm and hustled me through the crowd to the police station," she said.

"It is utterly absurd for these men (Long and Moon) to deny that I was under arrest. They realize now that they made a mistake and they are trying to get out of it. Why the sheriff even admitted to me that the arrest of my husband was a mistake."

The Syracuse newspaper provided its readers with a longer and more detailed account provided by Mrs. Lunn, who proved to any doubters on this day that she was far from being just a "parlor socialist."

"We came here this morning from Amsterdam where Mr. Lunn spoke Wednesday in the interest of his congressional campaign," Mrs. Lunn told the Herald. "We came here to be present at the hearing for Mr. Bakeman. Mr. Lunn had no intention of speaking at that time. When we arrived in Clinton Park, he commenced to talk to a number of people, more or less, who were present. He did not stand on the bench and only talked in a conversational way. A policeman stepped up to him and said something which I didn't get. Then the sheriff came up and spoke to him. Mr. Lunn was then arrested. Mr. Lunn had been reading from an editorial from a New York newspaper and when he was arrested he handed me the paper and requested me to read the article to the men. Then the sheriff came up to me and said, 'you can't read that.' I said, 'Won't you allow me to read it?' He said, 'no, you can not. Will you move on?' I replied that I would not, and then he said, 'you will have to come, too.' He took me by the arm and we walked up to the jail. I thought I was under arrest. I stayed in the recorder's office. After a while the sheriff came in and told me I might go to dinner at the Richmond and said he would go with me if I wished. We went to dinner and then I went back to the jail and saw Mr. Lunn. I came out and spoke to Mr. and Mrs. Wright, when a patrolman stepped up and told me I should not speak to anyone. That seemed all right, as I supposed I was under arrest. The sheriff then came and in the course of a conversation told me that I was not under arrest – I was glad of that, of course, but I am convinced that they intended to place me under arrest, but got cold feet and thought they had better not go farther. I never saw such a place. They do not seem to have any idea of what they are."

Moon, who by all accounts was polite and gentlemanly in manner, said he was only escorting Mrs. Lunn to the police station for her own safety. She was never, he stressed, under arrest. There was no debate as to her husband's status, and when Lunn appeared before Judge Collins he told him to treat him as any other "beaten man who might come before you without prestige."The judge did just that, sending Lunn and his six associates to the Herkimer County jail for the night on $1,000 bail, the charge "inciting to riot." The Gazette specified the offense, reporting that Lunn was charged with "refusing to leave a place of unlawful assemble after being warned by the officials to leave." Lunn could have afforded bail, but his comrades weren't blessed with wealthy in-laws, so the mayor decided to check out the accommodations at the Herkimer County jail in Rome. As Moon and his prisoners were leaving the Little Falls jail, a large crowd gathered and Lunn shouted at them, "I'll be back as soon as possible boys, and make another speech."

Before leaving the Little Falls jail that afternoon and heading to Rome, Lunn and the five men that were jailed with him, Bakeman, Simmons, DeGuerre, Louis Lenicke and Fred Hersh, composed a letter and gave it to Mr. Barry, who got it printed in the Syracuse newspaper on October 18.

"We, the undersigned citizens of the United States, in confinement in the miserable little jail of Little Falls because of our faith in the principles of the U.S. Constitution, Amendment 1, that the right of free speech should not be abridged, call upon decent and honest citizens, regardless of different opinions on other subjects, to join with us in our single demand that orderly and peaceful free speech be allowed in the city of Little Falls. We believed that no progress in the way of social amelioration or progress of any kind is possible without the right of free speech. We recognize that men have the right to strike against intolerable industrial conditions. When they strike they do not abrogate their rights as citizens. We have in this jail representatives of organized labor, both American Federation of Labor and Industrial Workers of the World. We have representatives of the Democratic Party, the Socialist Party and one worker who is not a member of any.

"Regardless of whether we are AF of L members, IWW members or as is the case with some, members of no labor organizations, whether we are members of one political party or no political party, we protest against the brutal treatment of the police and our absolutely unjust confinement. We especially protest against the brutal arrest of Mrs. George Lunn, who was guilty only of reading aloud an editorial from today's New York World, entitled "Our Rulers." The treatment we are receiving as citizens is the treatment of Russia, not that of the United States, as we have always thought it to be.

"We indignantly protest against the arrest of men quoting from Abraham Lincoln, reading from the Constitution of the U.S., and one of us for reading from the New Testament the words of Jesus.

"For I was hungred and you gave me no meat, I was thirsty and you gave me no drink, I was a stranger and you took me not in, naked, and you clothed me not, sick and in prison, and you visited me not. Verily I say unto you, inasmuch as you did it not to one of the least of these, you did it not to me."

During this time, Lunn was also a candidate for the U.S. Congress and had scheduled a campaign speech in Fort Plain on Friday night, October 18. Although still under arrest, Lunn was placed in Moon's custody and driven to Fort Plain, about 20 miles to the east. There he delivered a speech to a capacity crowd at the Fort Plain Theater. Mullen and Barry were already at the site and speaking when Lunn, accompanied by Moon, entered the place to a rousing ovation and took a spot on the stage. While some of Lunn's talk was about typical politics and the Socialist solution, he offered plenty of commentary about the recent events just up the Mohawk River in Little Falls.

"I am going to win the fight there, if I have to stay in jail the rest of my life," said Lunn. He also suggested that American Revolutionary War general Nicholas Herkimer, after whom the county was named, would turn over in his grave if he knew the conditions that existed there. At one point in Lunn's presentation, a deputy of Sheriff Moon's felt compelled to approach the stage and demand that Lunn stop talking and return to Rome. The crowd immediately went into an uproar, but Moon and other officials defused the situation by ushering the deputy outside the theater and making sure he was on his way to the nearby train station. Lunn summed up by thanking Sheriff Moon and the people of Fort Plain for their "utmost courtesy," and also predicted a victory in the November election.

Lunn and his fellow prisoners were released on Saturday, paroled without bail until the following Tuesday, October 22. On Saturday afternoon the mayor hurried back to Schenectady and that night spoke before a crowd The Citizen called the "largest assembly ever" in the city. While a sparsely-attended Bull Moose rally was going on in Crescent Park, Lunn attracted a large crowd to the corner of State and Barrett streets. The mayor was "worn out and only spoke a few words," reported The Citizen, which estimated the number of people at 10,000. While it might be safe to assume that the Socialist mouthpiece was a bit high with its crowd estimate, there's no question the large turnout impressed Lunn, who was also greeted by a huge throng when he got off the train from Little Falls.

"I regard the meeting at the New York Central depot as the greatest demonstration I have ever seen," said Lunn. "I am proud of Schenectady and I am proud to be the mayor of a city where any man has the right to speak on the streets or in the public park without molestation from the police, but with their protection. We are out on parole. We have to go back on Tuesday and I don't know what those people at Little Falls will do."

CHAPTER 17

Legal Battle Heats Up

The next morning Lunn delivered a sermon at the People's Church. That same Sunday the governor of New York, John Alden Dix, delivered his own sermon, by registered letter, to Little Falls and Herkimer County officials, reminding them about certain basic freedoms due their citizens. "Your attention is invited to the fact the Constitution of State of New York guarantees the right of free speech and the right of people to peacefully assemble and discuss public questions," wrote Dix, who Lunn had telegraphed on Monday asking for help. "The people of the State of New York wish to see that these rights are not unnecessarily curtailed, but are respected in spirit as well as in letter, within your jurisdiction."

Lunn was up early on Monday morning and back on the train to Utica. This time, when he began to speak at Clinton Park, sharing the stage with Socialist gubernatorial candidate Charles Edward Russell, there was a police presence but no move to interrupt the proceedings. Lunn and other Socialist orators were allowed to speak, giving the mayor a victory in his fight for free speech. However, the victory wasn't complete. The next day, Tuesday, October 22, most everyone expected Herkimer County D.A. Frank Schmidt to dismiss all charges against Lunn and his colleagues, but Schmidt had other ideas.

"These gentlemen came up here to be arrested and they succeeded," Schmidt said. "They are clamoring about free speech but that was only subterfuge to get them in jail and thus make political capital for themselves." Schmidt reduced the charge from a felony to a misdemeanor but told the court he was not dropping the charges. Judge Collins allowed Lunn and his counsel an adjournment until the following Wednesday, October 30. Lunn responded by saying he would never pay any fine for quoting Abraham Lincoln. Later that night, speaking in Amsterdam, Lunn told the crowd, "We fought them and we won. Today they allow free speech in Clinton Park to anyone. I am out on parole. We are to return next Wednesday. I know the cowards will hold us for the action of the grand jury for doing last week what they allow this week. Little Falls is a section of Russia not yet added to the Czar's domain. We intend to put it on the map of the U.S."

In other strike news, Schloss realized she could no longer serve in her capacity as visiting nurse for the Fortnightly Club. In a public statement dated October 17, she said, "The manufacturers have brought on the strike themselves by cutting down the wages almost to the starvation point. I know the life of these people, as perhaps no one else in town will ever know, and I feel that as a nurse and a social worker, it is my duty to sympathize with these poor strikers."

On October 24, workers voted at a mass meeting to join the IWW and submitted three demands to the mill owners: "Sixty hours pay for fifty-four hours of work; a 10 percent additional increase in wages; and no discrimination against workers for strike participation." On October 25 the striking workers held a parade and marched through the streets of Little Falls. A confrontation between the mostly immigrant strikers and the "American" workers at the Snyder Bicycle plant was avoided when a large police force arrived and separated the two groups, defusing a possibly violent encounter.

Following his adjournment on Tuesday, the 22nd, Lunn spent much of the next eight days on the campaign trail. He stumped for himself and Meyer London in New York City on October 27, spouting Socialist party politics while also sharing his experience in Little Falls. London, running for a seat in the U.S. House of Representatives from the 12th District, didn't win in 1912, but two years later became just the second Socialist (Victor Berger was the first) to be elected to Congress.

On Wednesday, October 30, Lunn was back in Little Falls for his court appearance, and by early afternoon he had been arraigned and put in front of a grand jury. His attorney, now Schenectady corporation counsel Frank Cooper, made a motion that the charges against his client be dropped, which Judge Collins denied. Cooper than explained that due to Lunn's busy schedule, no evidence in his defense would be offered that day, and Collins decided to push a trial date back to Nov. 15. With the approval of DA Schmidt, Lunn was not required to post bail and headed back east on the train to continue campaigning, the election being only six days away.

While Lunn and the Little Falls' legal authorities were playing nice in the court room, out on the street earlier in the day tensions had finally boiled over. John Andrews Fitch, a pioneering investigative journalist who wrote for the Pittsburgh Survey, visited Little Falls earlier in the month and had forecasted the trouble in a letter to the New York State Commissioner of Labor John Williams. The author of "The Steelworkers," a look at steel factory workers in Pittsburgh, Fitch said the Little Falls Police Department had expanded from just six officers to 90 with the influx of hired help, many of them from the Humphrey Detective Agency of Albany.

"They walked about in groups," reported Fitch, "carrying the clubs in their hands, and their attitude toward strikers and strangers upon the city streets is constantly menacing and evidently designated to intimidate."

Despite the presence of these "hired hands" or, you could argue, because of them, there had been no serious violence in Little Falls. But at 6:50 in the morning on that Wednesday, October 30, that all changed. Between 400 and 500 strikers, led by Bocchini, were parading peacefully at the Phoenix Mill No. 2, singing "Marseillaise," the popular French song Lunn had used to help celebrate his election in Schenectady nearly a year earlier. What happened next depends on who you believe. Chief Long claimed that he and about 20 policemen were watching the parade and that everything was peaceful until a few women employees on their way to work were prevented from entering the mill by the strikers.

"Here boys," the chief said, according to his account, "stop that, make way for the women if they want to go to work." The chief said he then received a blow to the head that stunned him for a moment, and by that time "the melee was on." Newspaper accounts differ as to the facts, and the Schenectady Union-Star, an evening publication, produced an article for its Wednesday edition that was supportive of Chief Long and the police. It's Thursday edition, however, presumably after a day of collecting more information, was much more sympathetic toward the strikers.

"Several shots were fired from the ranks of the strikers who closed in around the chief and his men, and the struggle became desperate," reported the Union Star on Wednesday evening, and the October 31 edition of the Schenectady Gazette wrote that "the strikers, with women at the front, closed in on the officers."

In his story on the riot later that month in the International Socialist Review, Phillips Russell reported that Chief Long had initiated the violence when "he prodded a young girl in the breasts with his club."

Regardless of how the violence began, the police response was quick and powerful as Long and his men were quickly aided by special police, some on horseback. James Kenney of Albany, part of the force from the Humphrey's Detective Agency, received several knife wounds and was taken to Little Falls Hospital, as was Little Falls' special policeman Michael Haley, who was shot in the leg. Many of the strikers also were hurt, and some were beaten unconscious by policeman wielding clubs. The strikers began falling back and crossed the Mohawk River looking for the safety of their own homes, but the police kept up their pursuit. After several arrests and a short lull in the action, around noon the police charged into the IWW offices at Slovak Hall in the foreign quarter and made more arrests. Bakeman and Schloss were among the 30 people arrested, while Legere spent the night in Utica but was arrested when he returned to Little Falls the next morning.

Bakeman was an active participant in the morning confrontation, while Schloss apparently was not, although Chief Long said that the nurse was arrested during the morning confrontation as she yelled "scab" at the female workers who were walking through the picket line.

Lunn, who was escorted to the train station by police and put on an east-bound train at 1 p.m., was happy to tell his version of events, printed in Thursday's newspapers.

"I consider my arrest for quoting Abraham Lincoln a detestable outrage, but the arrest yesterday of Miss Schloss while she was going to make soup for the strikers' children, I consider more detestable still," Lunn said in a written statement. "The strikers of Little Falls are without protection of law, which is to be deplored."

Lunn had apparently driven out from Schenectady that day in a car draped in an American flag.

"He [Schmidt] wanted to remove it, saying it made the car conspicuous," Lunn said. "It was not the city automobile. I told him there would be trouble if anyone removed the flag, and I also refused police protection as I thought I was in more danger from the police than from any other persons."

The Union-Star, after its rushed Wednesday report on the riot, gave plenty of room to the striker's version of events in its Thursday evening edition, and also reported that Haywood would soon come to Little Falls to contribute his considerable clout to the cause. The newspaper included several quotes from strikers telling their story, including one who said, "But the strike will not end. We are organized and we depend for sustenance upon our brethren in the labor ranks. We will bring Haywood and other leaders here, and we will fight all winter, if necessary."

The IWW issued a proclamation on Wednesday night, claiming the riot was caused by the Little Falls police and those hired to assist them.

"Today in Little Falls was seen a spectacle which has not been witnessed before anywhere outside of Russia," said the IWW. "Today the gang of fiends in human form who wear the disgraceful uniform of the police in Little Falls, deliberately went to work and started a riot."

It was Chief Long, said the IWW proclamation, who ignited the riot by clubbing Antonio Prete, a member of the strike committee, as he was walking alone in the middle of the street. When the strikers rushed to protect Prete from further abuse, the police also came rushing in and the fight was on. The IWW also said that the Little Falls policeman hit by a bullet, Michael Haley, was actually struck by fire from one of his colleagues.

"Let every lover of freedom and justice hear the cry of the opposed strikers of Little Falls," said the IWW. "Can these human brutalities be carried out with impunity in America?"

Haywood, writing for the International Socialist Review in early January, recounted how the IWW proclamation was not very well received by Little Falls officials.

"As soon as authorities found that the proclamation was being circulated, they went at once to Utica, 20 miles distant, arrested the printer, confiscated 3,000 of the proclamations and dragged the publisher to Little Falls, without warrant or authority where he was later released."

On Friday, November 1, The Citizen, the socialist voice in Schenectady, chimed in with its own reporting on the Little Falls trouble.

"That it was premeditated by the mill owners, executed by paid thugs, abetted by police and well advertised by the prostituted press throughout this region of the state is now as plain as day to all workers who have followed the history of the Little Falls strike.... The riot seems to be one of the most outrageous frame-ups in the history of the labor movement."

Lunn expanded on his earlier statement about Schloss's arrest in his own byline story in The Citizen that Friday, with the headline, "Sidelights of the Manufactured Riot."

Lunn backed up the IWW claim that the shooting of the officer was the work of one of his fellow policeman, and also mentioned the Humphrey Detective Agency, referring to them as "plug-uglies, whose business it is to incite to violence in time of labor troubles."

"The police and officials are determined to have violence," continued Lunn. "So determined are they that they allow mill owners to hire detectives and then the city officials appoint these detectives as special officers either under the police department or sheriff of the county".

Lunn's comments were not appreciated by William A. Humphrey, who sent out a statement from his headquarters at 467 Broadway in Albany defending his employees and the work they do. Humphrey called Lunn "crazy," and compared him and men like him to "dynamiters and law-breakers." A long-time chief of detectives for the New York Central Railroad who in 1906 was elected president of the Association of Railroad Police for the U.S. and Canadian Secret Service, Humphrey went on to say that the Schenectady mayor was the man most responsible for turning things violent in Little Falls.

"It is men like Lunn who are causing all this trouble today," he said in his statement, which was printed in full in the Little Falls Evening Times on Nov. 2. "You may put this as strong as you care to, for I mean it. If Lunn had been a law-abiding citizen and had remained at home, there never would have been any trouble at Little Falls. But he had to go there among the people, who until that time had acted peacefully enough and stir them up, excite them and incite them to violence. I say the fewer Lunns there are in the country, the better off this country will be."

While the strikers, the IWW and the Socialists were waiting for some support from the state's commissioner of labor, they didn't get it. The Evening Times reported on November 2 that Commissioner Williams believed firmly that the violence was the result of not the police or the strikers, but of the IWW and the Schenectady Socialists.

"As far as my information goes, the riots at Little Falls are directly attributable to the presence of outside disturbing elements," said Williams. "Before their arrival I believe it would have been possible to settle the strike through mediation, but now we are utterly unable to do anything."

Schloss and Bakeman and many of the other arrested strikers spent the next week in jail, with the "Little Red Nurse" occupying the same cell that once held convicted murderer Chester

Gillette before he was killed by electric chair in 1908 at Auburn Prison. Gillette had killed his girlfriend, Grace Brown, by beating her with a tennis racquet before tossing her body into Inlet Lake in the Adirondacks. It was a story that according to The Citizen and the New York Call, Schloss's jailors felt compelled to share with her.

Legere and Bocchini, meanwhile, also remained in jail. Taking over leadership of the strike was Robbins, and between her, Schloss, Haywood and some of IWW's most influential attorneys, the strike went on. Lunn, meanwhile, had an election to worry about.

CHAPTER 18

The Election

Much of the criticism hurled at the Schenectady mayor for his involvement in the Little Falls strike included the charge that he did it for political reasons. But, while it may have increased his profile around the state, whether or not it helped his chances at carrying the 30th district (which was made up of Schenectady, Fulton, Montgomery and Hamilton counties) and winning a seat in Congress isn't so clear.

There was so much going on during the fall of 1912 it was hard for a political office seeker to grab a headline. The country was absorbed by the four-way battle for president between the incumbent Republican William Howard Taft, the Democratic challenger Woodrow Wilson, the Progressive or Bull Moose candidate Theodore Roosevelt and Socialist Eugene Debs. And on October 14, as Roosevelt walked out of the Gilpatrick Hotel in Milwaukee on his way to a campaign event, he was shot by a bartender named John Schrank. A seemingly harmless individual most of his life, Schrank didn't believe any man should have three terms in office and, sparked by "the voice of William McKinley," he did his best to keep Roosevelt from returning to the oval office. Schrank aimed at Roosevelt's heart and very likely would have killed him if not for TR's glasses case, a bundle of manuscripts and the heavy coat he was wearing, all doing their part to slow down Schrank's 32-caliber bullet as it hit the area near his target's chest pocket. After Schrank was subdued – he was found to be criminally insane and spent the rest of his life in a mental hospital – Roosevelt continued on to his campaign stop and spoke for more than an hour before finally growing too weary to talk. He was rushed to the hospital where doctors informed him, as he had thought all along, that the wound was not serious.

Then on October 24, Vice President James Sherman, a Utica, New York native just 57 years old, died of complications from Bright's Disease, leaving the sitting president without a running mate two weeks before the election. Called "Sunny Jim" because of his friendly disposition, Sherman was the first vice-president to fly in a plane and the first vice president to throw out the ceremonial first pitch at a major league baseball game.

Back in Schenectady, Lunn spent the weekend speaking all over the city, county and region. On Friday, November 1, he was in Johnstown, and on Saturday he was heard by nearly 5,000 people during a Socialist Party celebration in Crescent Park. On Sunday afternoon he spoke in front of a Polish gathering in Schenectady, and that night the United People's Church secured Proctors Theater for a Lunn speech entitled, "The Struggle of the People Against Plutocracy." On Monday, the day before the election, he was back in Johnstown and Amsterdam, trying to dig up as many votes as he could where both Wallin and Reynolds figured to run strong.

Public debates between the contestants weren't a part of the 1912 campaign. Lunn didn't participate in any, and Wallin and Reynolds, not really your traditional politicians, also didn't seem that enthusiastic about trading ideas with their opponents in person. Reynolds used his Amsterdam newspaper as a mouthpiece for his campaign, and Wallin had the backing of the city's other newspaper, the Amsterdam Recorder.

"Dr. Lunn represents the forces of disorder and revolution," wrote the Recorder. "He stands for the red flag of socialism. Sam Wallin stands for the American flag and all it signifies."

The Bull Moose candidate, however, Professor Hale, did engage in a short impromptu debate with Charles A. Mullen, Lunn's Commissioner of Public Works, on a Saturday afternoon the previous weekend. The two men put on a wonderful display of splitting political hairs, much of which was probably lost on the crowd. When Hale took to the streets to share his opinion of the current administration in City Hall, Mullen appeared at the scene and began defending Lunn, trying to lure Hale into a discussion of the issues. Hale, however, went on with his stumping, criticizing Lunn's eagerness to bring in "imported" experts to help run the city, as well as questioning the hiring of the mayor's three Socialist secretaries (Lippman, Macy and Callery) who were "brought here avowedly and obviously in the interest of Socialist propaganda."

Hale went on to say that the Bull Moose or Progressive candidates were having their mantel stolen by Lunn and the Socialists.

"All the reforms advocated by socialism are advocated by the Progressives, who go even further," said Dr. Hale. "For instance, the Socialists believe in abolishing the United States Senate; we believe in the direct election of senators. As regards this policy, we have clear-cut socialism on one hand, and real reform on the other.

"I maintain if Dr. Lunn is sent to Washington it must be as a Socialist or as a reformer," continued Hale. "I believe Dr. Lunn would be a Socialist. The issue is clear. If he is to be elected in all sincerity, it must be by the Socialist vote. That is the constituency he represents. He knows as well as I and the rest of us that the Socialists can not elect him and for that reason he's preaching reform in the hopes of gaining the protest vote. Is he sincere and will he be a reformer or a Socialist in Washington? The Socialists believe in advancing the interests of the laboring class to the detriment of any other class. The Progressives do not believe in class interest; they believe that the interests of all classes should be common."

Mullen gained the crowd's attention long enough to remark to Hale, "You've been perfectly fair, doctor, with one exception. You claim that Dr. Lunn will represent the laboring class, but he'll represent the workers, and we are the workers."

"That's what Socialists would like to have people believe," said Dr. Hale in response, "but it is not what they really believe."

Lunn, who had spent Monday night in Amsterdam, was up early election day and back in Schenectady by 10 a.m. The ALCO workers enjoyed a beautiful day off according to the Gazette, while GE let all its employees leave at noon to perform their civic duty. At 10:55 that morning Lunn showed up at police court in city hall where Schenectadians in the Fourth Ward, 1st District voted for their candidate. The victory he was hoping for didn't materialize, but Lunn (the third-party candidate) could argue with some conviction that it was Hale (the fourth-party candidate) that kept him from winning a seat in the U.S. Congress. And the runner-up Reynolds, in more traditional election day politics, bemoaned how it was the third-party candidate that spoiled his chances.

While Hale's entry into the race for the 30th District probably did keep Lunn from carrying Schenectady County, in the overall picture it came down to the two Amsterdamians, with Wallin edging Reynolds by just 447 votes. The Citizen had attacked Wallin as a "millionaire businessman" who didn't care about the working conditions of the men, women and children that worked at his carpet mill, and his victory must have surprised the news and editorial staff at the Schenectady Gazette, which had declared in Tuesday morning's edition that the contest was strictly between the Democrats and the Socialists.

"Mr. Lunn in Congress," wrote the Gazette, "would be just about as potent (and no personal disrespect is meant by this comparison) as a flea in a herd of elephants."

The newspaper was right in one sense. In the voting inside the county, Reynolds, the Democrat, did prevail with 6,397 votes. Lunn was next with 5,839 votes, followed by Wallin's total of 4,662 and Hale's 1,844. While many politicians, most notably Wilson and Roosevelt, were battling for the progressive label, most Bull Moose or capital P Progressives took votes away from the Republican party. In Schenectady County, however, Hale's presence probably hurt Lunn more than it did Wallin.

In overall tallies from Schenectady, Montgomery, Fulton and Hamilton counties published in the Gazette the day after the election, Wallin had 14,150 votes, Reynolds 13,703 votes, Lunn 9,375 votes and Hale 4,663 votes. It was Wallin's numbers in

Fulton and Montgomery counties that helped him climb past Reynolds' superb showing in Schenectady County. Meanwhile, inside the City of Schenectady, Lunn finished a close second to Reynolds (5,097 to 4,894), and while he finished fourth (even behind Hale) in Fulton County, Lunn did carry the city of Johnstown, nudging Wallin, 717-681.

In Wednesday morning's newspaper, all the candidates seemed upbeat about the previous day's events. Wallin said in the Gazette, "The result in Amsterdam and Montgomery County is particularly gratifying. The flattering endorsement of my own townsmen pleases me more than anything else. The approval most worth having is that of a man's neighbor."

Reynolds was thankful for his showing in Schenectady County. "I feel unable to express my gratitude to the loyal friends who supported me in Schenectady County," he said. "The strength of the vote for Dr. Lunn, the Socialist candidate, was a surprise to many but not underestimated by me, for I took the brunt of the fight against the Socialist propaganda."

While the Gazette headline blared, "Wallin Thankful, Reynolds Pleased and Lunn Elated," the story was much less positive in reference to the Socialist candidate. "The mayor appeared as a man broken in health and spirit," reported the Gazette. "The campaign, with his executive duties and his troubles at Little Falls, have tolled materially on the man who a year ago entered the local political field in robust health and an iron constitution. To say the mayor has gone beyond his strength in endeavoring to fill his role as candidate, chief magistrate of a thriving municipality and minister of a gospel and free speech arbiter, is not exaggerating."

In his late Tuesday night interview with the press, Lunn did say that his loss was probably due to Hale's inclusion into the race, although his totals along with Hale's still would not have given him the victory. "The Republicans have no more right to claim the Progressives as a faction of their party than the Socialists have, for as far as the local Progressives go they will never again vote the Republican ticket," he said.

The Gazette article also reported how Lunn had "remarked that a year ago these same Progressives, with some exceptions, were his supporters at the polls. He declared their support this year would have given him his old vote," and thus sent him to the U.S. Congress. And, the Gazette added, Lunn was "elated" over his success in Johnstown. "It was where the Progressive ticket was least strong that the Socialists were the strongest," he said. "In Gloversville, the Progressives were strong, but in Johnstown they were not."

Election day in Schenectady wasn't without some controversy. Many voters in the first district of the Ninth Ward, the city's Mont Pleasant section, were disappointed when the polling place closed abruptly at 5 p.m. According to Wednesday's Gazette, the 150 voters inside the Congress Street school were allowed to cast their ballots, but the 50 or more outside were turned away. "Loud murmers of disapproval went up and the crowd began to push toward the door of the school building," reported the Gazette. Fearing a riot, officials called the city police to the scene and Sgt. Barney Magee of the Second Precinct told the crowd that the polls were officially closed. The crowd reluctantly went home. The Ninth Ward, a relatively new neighborhood in Schenectady, grew in population by 192.4 percent from 1910-1920, and the Poles and Italians that moved there, many of them recent immigrants who had found work at GE and ALCO, were most likely Lunn voters.

The mayor, however, didn't complain about the lost votes, and in Friday's Citizen, Lunn was much more positive about Tuesday's election results. He opened his own byline article by saying, "Socialism is never defeated," and that "the results of the election should fill every Socialist heart with joy."

Lunn also pointed out again that the Bull Moose Party had stolen many of his supporters.

"Our showing is splendid in face of the fact that 2,000 Bull Moosers who were with us last year are now in their own party."

As to the national election, Lunn was also pleased with the Socialist output.

"Nearly a million votes for Debs is good reason for rejoicing. Throughout this city and county and congressional district as well as the nation, Socialists are jubilant over the magnificent gains made by the party of the workers."

In the presidential election, two major issues were tariffs and women's suffrage. Woodrow Wilson, who back in July had won the Democratic nomination on the 46ᵗʰ ballot at the Baltimore convention, argued against tariffs and didn't address the women's vote, telling reporters it was better left to the states to decide. Taft, Theodore Roosevelt's conservative successor, was anti-suffrage and pro-tariff, giving his critics plenty of reason to refer to him as a pawn of big business, while Roosevelt himself was somewhere in between Taft and Wilson on tariffs, and in favor of women's suffrage. Debs, meanwhile, was a big proponent of a women's right to vote, and called the conversation over tariffs a "sham battle, an irrelevant issue when put alongside the more compelling problem of the plight of labor."

As many people expected, Roosevelt's inclusion into the race spoiled any chance of a Republican victory. Wilson won decidedly, gaining 42 percent of the vote while Roosevelt was next with 27 percent. The incumbent Taft was close behind his former friend with 23 percent of the vote, and Debs was a distant fourth, although his 900,672 votes gave him 6 percent of the total, marking the Socialist Party's highwater mark in American politics.

Debs had an even bigger impact in Schenectady County. In 1900, he had received just 32 votes for president, and in 1904 his tally jumped to 434 votes. In 1908, when Taft won over William Jennings Bryan, Debs collected 1,100 votes in Schenectady County, and in 1912 his total climbed to 3,456, which put him in third place among the candidates. Wilson led the way with 5,345, and Taft was second with 5,179. Roosevelt managed just 2,640 votes, putting the Bull Moose candidate, the runner-up nationally, nearly 1,000 votes behind Debs in the county. There was indeed enough cause to be optimistic about the future of Socialism in America, but Lunn's assertion that 1912 was another significant step forward for the party would prove to be wrong.

Herbert Merrill, who had been swept into the state assembly with the Lunn wave in 1911, also failed in his re-election bid to win another one-year term. In Milwaukee, the other "Socialist experiment" didn't go well. Seidel had lost his mayoral seat in the spring election of 1912, and in November Victor Berger, who had been the first Socialist to win a seat in the U.S. House of Representatives back in 1910, lost his re-election in Wisconsin's 5th district.

CHAPTER 19

Back to Little Falls

At noon Wednesday, November 6, the day after the election, Lunn and a group of local Socialists met at the mayor's office to determine their best course of action in Little Falls. They decided a strong show of support in the courtroom at Thursday's hearing for Legere, Bocchini, Schloss, Bakeman and nearly 30 strikers was in order. However, while Lunn and his entourage boarded an early-morning train for Little Falls on Thursday expecting a full day of legal theatrics, only Legere and three strikers were arraigned that day, and then held for the grand jury on the charge of assault in the first degree. The others, including Schloss, Bakeman and George Vaughn, would have their hearing on Friday.

"I came here today thinking that Miss Schloss, Mr. Bakeman and Mr. Vaughn were to be arraigned, but find that some of the other cases have been taken up first," Lunn told a reporter from the Little Falls Evening Times. "I did not think that they would keep Miss Schloss in jail all this time without giving her an examination."

Lunn, who took a seat alongside Legere for the courtroom's morning session, did not stay for the afternoon proceedings and did not return on Friday as Schloss, Bakeman and Vaughn were all arraigned and held for the grand jury, Schloss for inciting to riot, and Bakeman and Vaughn for first degree assault. After another night behind bars, bail was raised in the amount of $2,000 each for Bakeman and Schloss, freeing them from the confines of the Herkimer County jail. Several others, however, including Vaughn, Legere and Bocchini, remained imprisoned awaiting the grand jury.

It was a busy election week. While Legere was confined to the Herkimer County Jail on Thursday, the mill owners and the rest of Little Falls' business community held a big rally at the Hippodrome Theater "to take such action as may be deemed necessary at the time, for the preservation of peace, property and business stability and for the strict enforcement of the laws regulating riots and disorderly acts." Many of the city's most prominent citizens and other "Americans," as the Little Falls Journal and Courier put it, made up the large throng, supporting the mill owners as well as the police action headed by Chief Long. The weekly paper called the striking workers "quick-tempered" and "not well informed concerning American Institutions," and also took aim at the IWW, writing, "its leaders are dangerous characters, and its influence cannot be anything but harmful and dangerous. If the Little Falls exhibit is a fair sample of the whole organization, it should have the attention of the national government, and be thoroughly and effectively suppressed."

In Schenectady, the Gazette and the Union-Star were both hammering Mayor Lunn and the Socialist administration for sending city employees – police detective John Rooney and city dietician Margaret Wade – to Little Falls. Rooney came on Thursday accompanying Lunn, while Wade had been in Little Falls much of the week, running the soup kitchen for the striking workers while Schloss was in jail. "Citizens have raised the question," wrote the Gazette, referring in particular to Wade's week-long visit to Little Falls, "to her right to a salary here while in attendance with the strikers at Little Falls."

The week had begun with the arrival of Robbins, who, with Legere and Bocchini in jail, was directed by IWW headquarters in Chicago to head to Little Falls from Bridgeport, Connecticut, and assume control of the strike. A few days later, on Thursday, November 7, Haywood arrived and spent the next three weeks supporting the strike and inspiring the striking workers. He left on November 30, but it was Robbins who served as the primary organizer, fully demonstrating for the first time her value to the IWW leadership. When Legere was being arraigned on Thursday, a mass parade of striking workers, organized by Robbins, marched back and forth in front of the Little Falls Courthouse to show their support. Robbins, who stayed in an attic room of one of the strikers, was up and on the picket line at 6 a.m. each day with the strikers, and organized daily meetings at Sokol Hall and once-a-week social gatherings for dancing and singing. Robbins also visited the jail in Herkimer twice a week to consult with Legere, with whom she was romantically involved, and Bocchini. Robbins would spend 14 weeks in Little Falls, "perhaps the most memorable of my entire career as a labor organizer," she would write later.

On Friday, November 15, it was finally Lunn's time to learn his fate from the hands of Judge Collins. At 10:30 that morning, the mayor and his attorney, Frank Cooper, appeared in the Little Falls courtroom and were told by the judge that he, Lunn, was found guilty of violating a local ordinance. Lunn spoke out, "This is a question of principle and I will never spend a dollar for quoting Abraham Lincoln," bringing a short retort from Judge Collins, "The question of quoting Abraham Lincoln does not appear in the information that caused your arrest."

Before the judge could pass sentence, Cooper stood up and asked if the mayor would be allowed to make a short speech. City Attorney Newberry jumped to his feet, saying "I will object. We have had enough talk about the case and I don't want any newspaper acrobatics."

The judge initially denied the request. But when Lunn said, "the case against me was pretty well cut and dried," Schmidt barked, "It is not," and the exchange apparently changed Collins' mind. "I will give you two minutes to speak," said the judge. "We don't want to muzzle anyone."

Part of Lunn's remarks were published by the Little Falls Evening Times.

"I was not blocking traffic, or causing congestion," said the mayor. "I was going to address a peaceful assemblage. The prosecution is carrying in this case on a mere technicality and it is prejudiced. I was going to urge the men to use peaceful methods in their strike. I was quoting Abraham Lincoln when I was stopped. I have always advised peaceful methods and never a violent word has come from my mouth. I urged settlement of all cases on a basis of freedom. I did not resist arrest. I was seized and thrown into your jail."

When Lunn was done, Judge Collins told the defendant that the sentence was 50 days or $50. Cooper confirmed they had no intention of paying the fine and said they would appeal the case, and as a result Lunn was escorted to a waiting automobile and taken once again to the Herkimer County Jail. Cooper, irate that his client would actually have to spend another night behind bars while he prepared to file the papers for appeal, then questioned the court's fairness in its treatment of the other prisoners. Cooper charged that the arrested striking workers, many of them unfamiliar with the English language, had been railroaded through the court system and had unknowingly plead guilty to their various charges.

"If any more of these men are arraigned when I am not here there will be something doing," shouted Cooper, who was working for nine of the inmates, including Vaughn and Fred Hirsch, another Socialist from Schenectady whose only crime was that he had been escorting Mrs. Lunn when she had been detained.

"We can run this court without any one from Schenectady telling us how," said Collins. "We will not telephone to Schenectady every time a prisoner is arraigned. We have given these people from Schenectady decent treatment and they don't appreciate it."

"I am not telling the court what to do," said Cooper, "but I simply say what I will do."

"You go ahead and start anything you like," said Collins.

Lunn was escorted out of the courtroom by Chief Long, handed off to Sheriff Moon and then whisked away to Herkimer where he spent the night in a small six by eight foot cell. The next morning Lunn had breakfast in a common room with many of the strikers arrested for the rioting on October 30, and at one point led them in song. Lunn also tried to ease the anguish of Mrs. Walter Zugayka, who was in a nearby cell for alledgedly stabbing Officer Kenney. Not only was Zugayka distraught by her confinement and on the verge of collapse, her baby daughter had also been placed in the cell, adding to her emotional distress.

At noon that day, County Judge George W. Ward showed up in the Herkimer courtroom and was presented with Lunn's appeal. By 2 p.m. Lunn was released on $100 bond and was heading back to Schenectady with yet another court date, December 16. He spoke at the People's Church on Sunday morning, and then jumped on another train west to Utica where he shared the Lumberg Theatre stage on Sunday night with Haywood. The joint appearance of Lunn and Haywood and the questions it raised didn't go unnoticed by Schenectady's two newspapers.

"Mayor George R. Lunn, of Schenectady, yesterday astounded peacefully inclined, 'no violence' Socialists here by appearing upon and making a speech from the same platform as William D. Haywood, the notorious I.W.W. leader." The Union-Star went on to say, "With Lunn lined up with Haywood, say Socialists here, practically all pretense of his wing of the party in Schenectady standing for peaceful and lawful methods must be abandoned."

Another Union-Star article on the same page that day paraphrased what Lunn had to say about his Utica visit. "…the meeting was one of protest against the treatment of the Little Falls strikers and not in the interests of any labor organization," reported the newspaper. "The mayor said he did not appear as a representative of, or in affiliation with any organization, but merely in the interests of the strikers. Five of the strikers from Little Falls were present and took up a collection toward the support of their fellows, receiving about $100. Haywood, said the mayor, spoke briefly toward the end of the meeting."

Haywood's time in Little Falls was short and so was his time with the Socialist Party of America. He left Little Falls on the last day of November, and within two months was also out of the party, having been recalled from the group's national executive council in February. He remained an important part of the IWW, but in 1917 fled to Russia to avoid a 20-year prison term, having been convicted of "conspiring to hinder the draft, encourage desertion, and intimidate others in connection with labor disputes." The Espionage Act of 1917, trumpeted by President Wilson, enabled the government to charge Haywood and put an end to his labor career in the U.S.

Lunn, meanwhile, as reported by the Union-Star, was ready for a rest. Turning down an offer to speak in Baltimore, he stayed home for most of the week and no doubt read the newspapers, which were full of attacks on the Socialist Party. Charles A. Miles, one of the leaders of the American Federation of Labor, supported the Little Falls strikers but blamed Lunn and his fellow Socialists and the IWW for the violence and the failure to end the strike. Miles had come to Little Falls himself to witness first-hand what was happening, while Samuel Gompers, the founder and long-time president of the AF of L, was speaking in Rochester on November 19, calling the Socialists "disloyal" to the working class.

The week had also produced news from the Little Falls Evening Times forecasting that the strike would end soon, but that seemed like little more than wishful thinking by the newspaper. The arrest of two women on Wednesday, November 20, for throwing pepper at strike breakers suggested a different mood. Even though the newly-formed chapter of the AF of L announced that the strike had been settled on November 29, none of the foreign workers paid any attention and kept right on striking. While Miles had been successful in forming a small union affiliated with the AF of L, the United Textile Workers, Local #206, the group only had about 100 members and almost all of them were Irish from a neighborhood in the northern section of Little Falls. So, while Little Falls' only daily, the Evening-Times, had declared the strike over and trumpeted the efforts of the AF of L in finding a solution to the strife, it was very clear as the month of December opened that the strike wasn't over, and that it was Robbins and Schloss who were in control.

On December 3, even the Evening Times conceded as much.

"On the other hand, followers of the IWW say they know nothing of a settlement," reported the Little Falls newspaper.

"There was a largely attended meeting in Slovak Hall on Sunday, with Miss Rabinowitz, the girl leader from Bridgeport, Conn., in charge. There were several speeches in Italian and Polish and the keynote of all was stand firm. Miss Rabinowitz gave out a statement in which she refuted the charge that the IWW leaders are profiting by the trouble: that the leaders are not stopping at the Richmond, but are given food and shelter in the homes of the strikers, and that all funds coming into her hands will be reported in detail when the strike is settled."

The newspaper also quoted Schloss in depth.

"We have been working for the strikers for seven weeks and some of us have been beaten and thrown into jail," she said. "After we have sacrificed so much, it seems unjust for another organization [the AF of L] to come in at the last minute and attempt to snatch the glory of a victory. The strikers have learned to organize and have learned what they want. The IWW has taught the workers what the church is trying to teach them, love for their fellow man, without regard to their race or color."

While Robbins and Schloss kept busy in Little Falls, Lunn was back in Schenectady taking care of city business. After a few days at home, he went back on the road, but his focus had shifted away, if only for a while, from Little Falls. On Saturday, November 23, he left Schenectady for the Midwest where he had speaking engagements in Chicago, Cleveland and Milwaukee. The purpose of the trip was to see what these large municipalities were doing with their garbage, and William J. Springborn, the President of the Board of Public Service in Cleveland, was among those advising Lunn. An expert in trash collection who helped create the nation's first aluminum recycling plant in Cleveland a few years earlier, Springborn had gained some notoriety a few years earlier for having lost $10,000 betting on a wrestling match that had been fixed by corrupt promoters. While he didn't know much about wrestling, he did know garbage, and his expertise on the subject made him a valuable source of information to officials in other cities such as Schenectady that were looking into the relatively new world of trash collection. In fact, Springborn had already been to Schenectady in November to offer some advice before Lunn headed out to the Midwest to see the Cleveland operation first hand.

His trip was highlighted by a speech before a large Socialist gathering at the Garrick Theater in Chicago on Sunday, November 24, an event that was covered by the Chicago Tribune. Lunn couldn't help but bring up the strike in central New York. "The Little Falls strike is for bread," he said. "There isn't a rich man in Chicago who doesn't keep his horses better than the strikers of Little Falls are kept." Lunn's by now often-used refrain about refusing to pay any fine for quoting Lincoln was well received, and he went on to tell his audience about his administration's ventures into the coal and ice businesses. On Monday, Lunn spoke in Milwaukee, and he happily reported to the Union-Star when he got back home on Wednesday night that he had raised $166 in Chicago and $56 in Milwaukee for the striking workers.

Along with Lunn's financial contribution, the strikers also got a financial and spiritual gift from Helen Keller. On Friday, November 29, a Thanksgiving message from Keller was read to them by John Macy, Lunn's former secretary and still an avid Socialist who visited Little Falls to support the cause. In a meeting at the Slovak Hall the day after the holiday, Macy got up in front of a large group of striking women, read Keller's letter and presented the strike committee a check for $87.

"I am sending the check which Mr. Davis paid me for the Christmas sentiments I sent him," wrote Keller, explaining her financial contribution. "Will you give it to the brave girls who are striving so courageously to bring about the emancipation of the workers at Little Falls?

"They have my warmest sympathy," said Keller's letter. "Their cause is my cause. If they are denied a living wage, I also am defrauded. While they are industrial slaves, I cannot be free. My hunger is not satisfied while they are unfed. I cannot enjoy the good things of life which come to me, if they are hindered and neglected.

"Surely the things the workers demand are not unreasonable," said Keller. "It cannot be unreasonable to ask of society a fair chance for all. It cannot be unreasonable to demand the protection of women and little children and an honest wage for all who give their time and energy to industrial occupations. When indeed shall we learn that we are all related one to the other, that we are all members of one body? Until the spirit of love for our fellowmen, regardless of race, colour or creed, shall fill the world, making real in our lives and our deeds the actuality of human brotherhood – until the great mass of the people shall be filled with the sense of responsibility for each other's welfare, social justice can never be attained."

CHAPTER 20

December, 1912

As busy as he was in October and November, Lunn showed no signs of slowing down in December. On Sunday, the first of the month, the mayor was in Philadelphia and more impassioned than ever, again telling the story of the Little Falls strikers. Speaking at the Broad Street Theatre, he remarked how he would never "pay a cent to the treasury of Herkimer County, New York for using the words of Lincoln." In the Gazette's story reporting Lunn's speech, the newspaper scolded the mayor with the headline, "The Minister-Mayor Quoted as using Profanity on Sunday in Quaker City." Talking about Judge Collins and his upcoming court date in Little Falls, Lunn had told his Philadelphia audience, "I don't give a damn what he says. I'll go to jail before I pay that fine."

On December 3, still in Philadelphia, Lunn spoke at the Municipal Progress Dinner and argued that all of society, the rich, the middle class and the poor, should be working together for the common good.

"If we can, through our municipalities, reduce the cost of such necessities as coal, ice, water and electricity, gas and transportation, it is in the interest of all of us to do it," said Lunn. "I am so much a believer in fundamental justice that what is for the best interest of the majority, the great mass, will prove eventually to be for the best interest of all of us."

Lunn was back in his office at the City Hall Annex in Schenectady on Thursday, Dec. 5, and on Friday afternoon he was paid a visit by Schloss and Charles Rowe, the losing Socialist candidate for the state assembly from Montgomery County. Those three were joined by Bakeman and other members of the Socialist local to determine what role Schenectady would play in the strike in the coming weeks. Meanwhile, that same day in Little

Falls, Robbins released a long, detailed account of the strike in which she asked Gov. Dix to call in the state militia on behalf of the strikers.

"The peace of Little Falls was never disturbed until the mill owners brought in a gang of thugs and gunmen from Albany," wrote Robbins, who was now referred to as the secretary of the Little Falls defense committee. "These men were supplied by the Humphrey Detective Agency of Albany, and on their arrival in Little Falls were sworn in as special policemen by the chief of Little Falls police, who, from the beginning, has been bitterly hostile to the strikers and the foreign population of the city generally.

"The very next morning after their arrival," continued Robbins' statement, referring to the violence on October 30, "these private detectives, led by the Chief of Police, deliberately and murderously attacked the strikers who were peacefully parading. The police, using their clubs and guns, injured scores of strikers, both women and men, shot one policeman by mistake and shot one bystander in the head, who was not a striker but happened to be a foreigner. They then arrested all four organizers, speakers and members of committees, preferring against them false charges of assault, thus hoping to break the strike."

Robbins also mentioned that the striking workers, about 1,000 of them, had joined the IWW local, that "our methods were absolutely peaceful," and that "they desire to remain peaceful." Robbins added that "at no time has there been any kind of clash between the strikers and the workers still remaining in the mills."

Dix, a native of Glens Falls about 50 miles north of Schenectady, deliberated over the IWW statement on Saturday and Sunday, and then Monday's newspapers reported his decision. The governor, a Democrat with less than a month left in his one two-year term, declined to use the state militia in Little Falls.

Lunn, battling on many fronts, also suffered a setback. On that same Monday night, the mayor's initial efforts to create a city park were defeated in the Common Council by an 8-5 vote, one vote short of the two-thirds needed for success. The mayor's plan included a $800,000 bond levied on the taxpayers, and while it might have been hard to vote against parks and playgrounds for children, the Socialists couldn't convince one of the opposition on the city council to vote with them. When Alderman Dunn from the first ward, the same person who proposed the anti-flag resolution back in May, voted no, securing the bond's defeat, the city hall chambers, packed mostly with Socialists, erupted in anger. Lunn, who had addressed the large assembly before the vote in a "mild, paternal manner," according to the Gazette, grabbed the floor again after Dunn delivered the bad news and "spoke in threatening terms, rebuking the minority for not voting with the administration," and informing the five dissenters that he would continue to put the park plan up for a vote at every City Council meeting.

"If they want politics," said Lunn, heatedly, "we will give them politics." The mayor thought it peculiar how some of the city's wealthy "businessmen had favored the widening of Lafayette Street because it would aid city businesses, yet they wished to deprive people the healthful benefits of parks."

Lunn pointed a finger at Dunn and one other alderman he said were pressured to vote against the park plan.

"I believed there were at least two alderman who were bigger than the political henchman who holds them in his grasp," Lunn told the Gazette. "I have been elected to carry out the will of the people, and I know what the will of the people is."

Lunn also suggested that Alderman Dunn does not represent the people that elected him. The Gazette, usually the Democrats' mouthpiece, gave the Republican an opportunity to defend his actions. Paraphrasing Dunn's response, the paper reported that, "Alderman Dunn denied that pressure had been brought to bear on him. He reminded the mayor that he [Dunn] had been elected by the people of the First Ward, who had repudiated him and his party, and that he was voting as he thought his constituents wanted him to vote."

Steinmetz, who was Lunn's pick to head the park board, also offered his view to reporters after the meeting.

"I speak because I know the citizens are overwhelmingly in favor of the park issue," he said. "There is a small minority against parks. Of those opposed you will find none of the ministers, none of the physicians, all of whom know the inestimable value of parks to the health of the city. You will find among the opposition none of the working men and their associations, for they know that parks are of great value to the workingman. Among those opposed you will find none of the faculty of ancient Union."

Politicians were the main culprit according to Steinmetz, and people that have "opposed all progressive movements in the past, who opposed asphalt pavement because they thought cobblestones were good enough, and who opposed the driving out of typhoid because they had become accustomed to drinking mud and water from the river and spring water from the cemetery.

"The minority," summed up Steinmetz, "will block anything the Socialists will try to do."

While the city council would tussle with the park issue several times in the next few months, there were other problems with which Lunn was dealing with. He was looking into the workings of the Schenectady Railway Company and the ongoing "six tickets for a quarter" fight that started between the city and the trolley car bosses long before Lunn took office, and he was still gathering information on garbage disposal as well as the city's water supply.

The third week in December opened with the press reporting on Monday that Schloss had decided to leave Little Falls and move to Amsterdam. Earlier in the month, before visiting Lunn in Schenectady on December 6, Schloss had been arrested when trying to speak in Clinton Park and was either pushed, tripped or fell down a stairway at the police station. Some accounts said Chief Long was the culprit, others said it was two of his men. The Little Falls Journal and Courier, the city's weekly newspaper, reported that Schloss had "stumbled, and the chief did not lay hands on her as witnesses can testify."

The Citizen, however, reported in its Friday, December 6 edition that Schloss "was set upon by two officers and thrown down the stairs of the police station on Monday," and on Wednesday "was subjected to further indignities." Whatever the truth, she apparently felt her time in Little Falls had come to an end, and among Socialists and her other friends there was genuine concern for her well being. In that same edition of The Citizen, Bakeman added his own strong rebuke of the Little Falls police.

"I know what I have seen from my own eyes that the treatment of Helen Schloss by the authorities in Little Falls is disgraceful," said Bakeman. "Has an aroused public indignation any means of expressing itself or must it stand helpless and dumb while a brave woman suffers insults and abuses from a tyrannical police power. Is there any legal authority that can guarantee protection to a brave woman giving her best to the exploited workers. If there is not some of us want to know at once."

While Schloss was in Amsterdam with Rowe, Lunn and Bakeman had to hurry to Herkimer on Tuesday, December 17, at the order of DA Schmidt. As both men expected, they were again indicted, but when Cooper made a motion to defer the plea until he could make a formal motion before Supreme Court Justice Andrews in Syracuse, Judge Ward allowed it and set a December 24 date for Lunn to return to court. Lunn remained free on his own recognizance and Bakeman on bail, but neither were reportedly happy about having to travel all the way to Little Falls just to be formally indicted. Bakeman had been in bed in Schenectady for three days, suffering from inflammatory rheumatism in his left leg, and was seen using a cane at the train station. His condition was apparently due to his repeated visits to the Little Falls Jail.

The cases of Lunn and Bakeman were handled without incident that day, and Schloss actually had some good news, the court deciding not to indict her on the charge of inciting to riot. Not everything went smoothly for Schmidt, however, who had just two weeks left in his term, having lost his re-election bid in November. As Carlos Ferrali, one of the strike leaders, was being arraigned, attorney A.D. Thomas of Herkimer announced to the court that his client was asking "that the indictment charging him with assault in the first degree be withdrawn and he is willing to plead guilty to assault in the third degree."

Bakeman, aware that Ferrali had little understanding of English, let Cooper know he was suspicious with the proceedings, and Cooper was also a bit uncomfortable with what was going on, remembering that his similar attempts to get charges reduced just a few weeks ago had been routinely dismissed. When Judge Ward directed that Ferrali be questioned through an interpreter, the defendant was asked, "you plead guilty?" According to The Citizen, when Ferrali answered, "why should I plead guilty? I didn't do anything," his response elicited "a silent uproar in court." Then, when Thomas attempted to take the man everyone presumed to be his client and leave, Bakeman again interceded and as a result Ferrali left for a consultation with IWW lawyer Fred H. Moore and Little Falls attorney Richard A. Hurley, who were working with Cooper. Ferrali told the two men that Thomas had approached him uninvited and that he had not retained Thomas as his attorney.

For The Citizen and anyone sympathetic with those arrested in connection with the strike, the actions by Thomas did not go unnoticed. The Schenectady weekly also pointed out that the foreman of the Little Falls jury, Henry Collins, was apparently a close friend and business associate of the mill owners. Manager of the electric power company that services the Little Falls area, Collins was known to have, according to The Citizen, fired an employee for being in sympathy with the strikers. It was all information that didn't bode well for the state's case, and very likely wasn't going to pass muster in Syracuse in front of Justice Andrews. The Citizen reported that Andrews was not a "partisan of the workers in the class struggle, but he has a great reputation as an incorruptible lover of equal justice as he sees it, and it was certain from the start that he would not be a party to any Little Falls deals."

On the same day that Lunn and Bakeman were heading west to Herkimer, a train from Little Falls was traveling east toward Schenectady with 18 children on board. Back on November 28 Schloss told the Evening Times that while many offers had been received, there were no immediate plans for the strikers' children to go anywhere, the intention being to "keep all the families intact until it becomes expedient, as a measure of economy and to ensure their comfort, to send the children away."

But on that Tuesday, December 17, a small number of parents were willing to have their kids taken away to what they hoped was a much safer place. The idea had worked well in terms of creating public sympathy for the strikers in Lawrence, Massachusetts earlier in the year when the children were taken all the way to New York City. As in that occasion, newspapers ran plenty of photographs of the youngsters leaving their families at the rail station or huddled together just off the train in their new temporary home, waiting to see where they would go next.

At noon that day, when the whistle blew telling GE and ALCO workers it was time for lunch, many women headed over to City Hall with soup and sandwiches, knowing that the children would be arriving soon. After the train pulled into the station just before 1 p.m., the new visitors were hustled over to the makeshift cafeteria set up at the City Hall Annex. After being fed and given some new clothes, the 18 children were distributed among the citizens of Schenectady and taken into private homes. Both the Gazette and the Union-Star reported how "none of the prominent Socialists in the administration took any of the children."

City treasurer Philip J. Andres, an ardent Socialist, responded to the two newspapers.

"They were right," said Andres. "No one is prominent in the Socialist Party. We're just comrades."

While the strikers' children were mostly taken in by Socialist families, there was plenty of Christmas spirit being spread around Schenectady that week. The city and its churches offered free lunches and clothing to the indigent at various venues throughout the days leading up to December 25, and on Saturday, December 22, the good feeling was heightened even more when Andrew Reid, a young teenage boy, saved the life of 8-year-old Jennie May Thorne. The young girl had been playing on the frozen pond at the Wendall Avenue quarry and had broken through the ice. Reid, playing hockey with some friends nearby, heard her screams and ran to help. After lying down on the ice, Reid extended his "shinney" stick to Jennie May, who grabbed hold and was pulled out of trouble by her rescuer and his young friends. While Reid's performance was the best of the weekend, for some Socialists Matilda Robbins's speech at the People's Church was a close second.

She and Schloss had been speaking in several cities around the state raising money for the striking workers, and according to Charles W. Wood, a columnist for The Citizen, her impassioned plea for help was inspirational. "In a wonderful address coming straight from the heart," wrote Wood, "the girl moved her hearers as few finished orators in the world could do." As she shared her Little Falls experience and spoke of the workers' plight, Robbins was at times on the verge of tears. Her appearance raised $143 for the strikers' fund, and Wood was enthralled by the "delicate little Russian girl," wondering why the other churches in Schenectady that day could not see the need to contribute some of their own offering.

"I do not know what this little girl's religion is," wrote Wood. "I do not know whether she has any of the labeled religions. I do not care. But I would like to know if the Christian ministers in Schenectady can stand unmoved before a situation which overpowers her.

"Whatever the church may think of the IWW," continued Wood, "is there not one church in town, except the United People's, which has a word of encouragement to these men and women and children who come to this country in blooming health and are reduced in a few short months to consumptives and starvelings by our glorious profit system in America?"

Wood went on. "Isn't there one other church that will say: 'Go to it, fight to the limit for your manhood, your womanhood and your childhood.... If not, why should any workingman be interested in the church?"

CHAPTER 21

More Troubles

With an optimistic eye toward Little Falls, the heroic rescue of Jennie May Thorne and Robbins's inspirational speech at his church, Lunn must have been upbeat as Christmas week arrived. However, as 1912 drew to a close, any positive feelings Lunn was experiencing quickly dissipated and were replaced by a series of woes, one quite tragic.

At Monday night's Common Council meeting, the five minority alderman again voted against the park issue, arguing that while the creation of a new park system wasn't a bad idea, Lunn's initiative at this time was just too expensive for the city. The minority did announce, however, that they would propose a compromise ordinance at the next meeting that would create new parks for a much smaller sum.

Along with problems from the minority on the council, Lunn also had serious troubles with members of his own party. Burns, the 13th ward alderman and a Socialist, had formed a committee within the Socialist local, and at what the newspapers were calling a "secret Socialist meeting" on Tuesday night, some of Lunn's comrades were charging the mayor and members of his administration with misappropriating city funds. Burns and his "investigating committee" reported that city money had been used to pay employees of George R. Lunn Associates during the mayor's venture into the ice business, and in a related matter the work of street superintendent Jim Hickey, a Lunn appointee but not an avid enough Socialist for some, was also brought into question. Burns suggested that the party should dismiss Hickey for various offenses, including violation of the state's eight-hour law and "discourteous treatment of city employees." The debate went long into the night, and Lunn, after remaining quiet for most of the evening, rose to tell his fellow Socialists, reported the Gazette, "the local had no authority over the superintendant and that if anyone was going to be recalled it would be he, the superintendent's superior and sole sponsor for the acts of the administration." Lunn's firm hand, according to the Gazette informant, "brought about a change, resulting in a censure instead of a dismissal." The meeting lasted until after 1 in the morning on Christmas Eve, but except for the powerless "censure" of Hickey, nothing was accomplished other than sowing the seeds of party disharmony that would erupt later in Lunn's two-year term.

The Schenectady County Progressive Association, meanwhile, had addressed an open letter to the Common Council on Monday night registering its concern about the cost of the new park system proposed by the Lunn administration. The Union-Star took this action to mean that the Progressives, typically an informal, loosely-knit group of disaffected Republicans and Democrats in the city, were planning to present a strong challenge for the mayoral seat in the 1913 election in the fall. This, warned the Union-Star, was a mistake.

In a news article quoting an anonymous source – "a prominent Progressive"– the newspaper argued how only a "non-partisan anti-Socialist city movement" could oust Lunn from office in November. Speaking to the Union-Star, he said, "in his mind, the party would be making a big mistake to put a ticket in the field next fall, as their vote at the last election was not such as to give rise to any belief in permanent party strength." An unnamed Democrat interviewed by the Union-Star also said that "the party had no official election organization, that it could not conduct a campaign against a united and fanatical enemy, and as the Progressives were forbidden to endorse the candidates of any other party, their assumption that either of the old parties would endorse Progressive nominations seemed to him to be the height of imprudence based on crass political ignorance."

A headline with the story proclaimed, "Forces of Good Government to Unite in War on Fad and Fanatics," and the article went on to say, "Let Democrats, Republicans, Progressives and Prohibitionists all join in the movement with a mixed ticket," and that only "a ticket selected after conference between all anti-Socialist leaders and put forward without any brand of party would rescue the city next fall."

In the December 24 issue of the Gazette, the newspaper reported that five of the civil service stenographers at City Hall were "being forced to write out 65 pages of testimony which was taken in Little Falls in Mayor Lunn's case." The paperwork was to be used by Lunn when he appeared in a Syracuse court on Christmas Eve, but it was Cooper who headed west that day and made a motion to inspect the grand jury minutes from the Little Falls trial. Collins adjourned the case and said he would make a decision on Lunn's request on December 31.

On Christmas Day, a Wednesday, Lunn got up, read his morning newspaper and came across a long editorial in the Gazette with the headline, "The Administration and the Park Question." It pointed out, quite fairly it should be mentioned, that everyone voicing an opinion against the administration's proposal wasn't necessarily against parks. "It implies that any dissent from its ideas and plans is an attack on the general proposition of securing parks," wrote the Gazette. The editorial went on to say that while it is very likely most Schenectadians did indeed want a park system, "some of those who earnestly favor them [parks] do not endorse the plans of the administration as presented."

Then, in the early morning hours of December 26, in the midst of all this political and civic turmoil, a hotel on the corner of State Street and Washington Avenue was gutted by fire and took the lives of two residents. For the next two weeks, the Freeman House fire was on the front page of the Gazette and the Union-Star, both newspapers questioning how and why the fire started, and both trying to assign blame. Lunn promised a complete investigation, and following a conference with State Fire Marshall Thomas J. Ahearn, Schenectady Fire Chief Henry R. Yates and Schenectady's Commissioner of Public Safety John E. Cole on Friday, January 1, 1913, some changes in building codes were made as was clarification of just who would enforce the guidelines. The fatal flaw at the Freeman House that night was the lack of fire escapes, as well as a government bureaucracy that made it hard to lay blame precisely on any particular entity. In the end, the already maligned Schenectady Railway Company – still fighting the city about its fares – was the main culprit in the Freeman House fire because it owned the building. The city's building inspector had informed the owners that the Freeman House failed to meet certain requirements, but didn't feel compelled to press the issue and make them comply. According to the Union-Star, the Schenectady Railway Company had suggested that they were soon going to close the building, and as a result that's why they took no action.

"There can be no effective enforcement of the law regarding fire escapes where there is any question as to who has the authority," Lunn told the press on December 30. "No man can be held responsible for the enforcement of a law unless he has such authority. There seems to have arisen a question as to authority in specific cases. These matters will be settled and settled at once. Strictest enforcement will follow."

Lunn and Cole both promised that much closer inspection and enforcement would keep tragic fires to a minimum in the future, and the administration also decided to put more responsibility in the hands of the fire chief, as well as create an assistant's position to the building inspector.

As to Little Falls, things were happening. Governor Dix, in one of his final acts as governor, did recommend mediating a solution to the strike. On Friday, December 27, three members of the State Board of Mediation and Arbitration began taking testimony from the striking workers. Almost all of the strikers were examined through an interpreter, were under 23 years of age, and all complained about their wages. Those working at night said they were ordered to put in 13-hour shifts with just one 30-minute break for lunch. By late Monday afternoon, Dec. 30, the board had wrapped up its work, listening not only to striking workers, but also those who had left the strike and gone back to work. Also among those giving testimony was Chief Long, who told the board that he had only defended himself in the rioting, and that his orders to the police were not to use clubs except in self-defense. In its evening edition on December 31, the Union-Star reported that the state board had determined that "outside agitators were responsible for the strike in Little Falls," but that the goal of the board was to help settle the strike and not force any binding resolution on either party.

"It is not its purpose to make a decision or determination," reported the newspaper, "but to use its endeavors to settle the strike, as its powers in the matter are entirely advisory."

In the same article, it also reported that both "John F. McLaughlin and Judson Gilbert, managers of the principal mills involved in the strike, today indicated their willingness to take back any of their former employees, and said that they should not be discriminated against because of the part they had taken in the strike. They are firm in their belief that the strike would have been ended long ago but for what they denominate outside interference."

McLaughlin, however, also told reporters "that he would positively refuse to deal with the IWW, which he referred to sarcastically as the 'I Won't Work.'"

On New Year's Eve morning, Cooper, acting as Lunn's counsel, took the train west past Little Falls to Syracuse where he had an afternoon meeting with Justice Andrews to discuss Lunn's motion to inspect the Herkimer County grand jury minutes. While the mayor stayed home in Schenectady with his family, Cooper argued that Lunn's constitutional rights of free speech had been violated by the Little Falls Police.

The Utica Observer Dispatch sent a reporter to the courtroom who supplied a lengthy summation of the proceedings, including "Mr. Cooper maintained that no legislature, common council or police officer had the right to stop free speech as long as there was orderly conduct, and that if the action of the Little Falls authorities was upheld the right of free speech anywhere in the country was jeopardized."

Cooper claimed that it was not his client who disturbed the peace and incited a riot, but the Little Falls police themselves.

"Everything which occurred in the way of disorder happened, Mr. Cooper said, after the police stopped Mr. Lunn from speaking," reported the Observer-Dispatch. "Up to that time it had been an orderly assemblage."

According to the December 31 Syracuse Journal, "the motion to inspect is on the grounds that the evidence was insufficient, illegal and incompetent, and a violation of the law governing grand juries. If it is granted, a motion to dismiss the indictment will be made."

While Cooper was probably expecting to argue his point against Schmidt, the Herkimer County district attorney took off what was his last day in office. When Herkimer attorney James H. Greene, standing in for Schmidt, requested that Andrews make an immediate determination on Lunn's motion because "Schmidt went out of office at midnight," Andrews responded, "in that event, Mr. Schmidt's successor would probably take care of the matter."

The justice, not wanting to be hurried into a decision, said he would have to give the case longer consideration, and gave Schmidt and Greene a January 7 court date for his ruling on whether or not Lunn would get a look at the grand jury minutes.

While 1912 had come to an end with a lot unsettled, Lunn must have felt optimistic about the future. In Albany, a new Democratic governor, William Sulzer, was about to take over and supported the same progressive issues as Lunn and most other Socialists, such as direct election of senators and woman's suffrage. That week in Canajoharie, also on the Mohawk River just east of Little Falls, officials at Beechnut, a large producer of baby food, announced that the company would award a $3 bonus for each year of service to every employee. In addition, they would also begin a reserve fund to help employees dealing with work-related accidents and establish a death benefit. Things did seem to be changing. As for Lunn and his activities in Little Falls, the mayor had done just about everything he could to help the striking workers, and a positive outcome seemed imminent. His own legal proceedings were still up in the air, but there too Lunn must have felt hopeful.

In Schenectady, GE and ALCO were both operating in high gear as immigrants continued to flow into the city looking for jobs. If Lunn had any reason for disappointment or despair after completing his first 365 days as mayor, it was probably in his own camp. The local Schenectady Socialists were not a singular group by any means, with each ethnicity having its own chapter. For Socialists, the devil was in the details, and arguments over policy and patronage continued to plague the organization. And, on a grander scale, the division between the ranks, the distinction between the political actionists and the direct actionists, was growing. While men like Lunn were willing to fight within the system to change the world, others such as "Big Bill" Haywood believed more drastic measures were the only option left for the poor working class. Both camps had an uphill battle. G.K. Chesterton, the English writer, orator and Christian apologist who debated the merits of socialism with staunch supporters such as George Bernard Shaw, said in December of 1912 that socialism had its inherent weaknesses, just like every other political viewpoint. "As to the distribution of property, the Socialists have a good idea, but no one now trusts the Socialists; they have become politicians, and no one trusts a politician."

CHAPTER 22

1913

In The Citizen on Friday, January 3, Lunn authored a column trumpeting the end of the strike in Little Falls.

"The discovery of power and breath of temporary freedom has opened a new world to the exploited men and women of Little Falls," he wrote. "They will never again be what they have been in the past. They will rise to greater strength, and firmly organized will recognize their own power and develop accordingly."

Two days earlier in Little Falls, Matilda Robbins and Fred H. Moore, the IWW attorney, had suggested to a mass meeting of workers at the City Theatre that it was time to head back to the mills. The mill owners, through the state mediation board, had agreed to most of the workers' demands, including: all men and women working 54 hours to receive the pay formerly received for 60 hours, an increase of 15 percent in the price for piece rates, and an hour of lunch was granted for those working the night shift. Also, there would be no discrimination against individual strikers, and the company agreed to reinstate all former employees as soon as possible.

Moore told the strikers at the New Year's Day meeting that whatever action they take today, "the fact remains that when they go back into the mills, the industrial struggle with their employer is again renewed." He added that they may go back to work "untrammeled by any contract or restraint, your only obligation being, so far as the terms are concerned, that they are accepted for that day and for that day only. If 48 hours or 72 hours later you believe that the time is right for a higher wage scale then it is for you to determine it at that time. You go back not bound up in a contract or agreement."

Before calling for a vote, Robbins told the strikers: "I have been speaking for nine weeks and I am going to take a rest. The terms have been explained to you. No matter if you settle or don't, you will be victorious because they have recognized that you are a compact body, and have something to hold to and something to hold you together. You know how to work together if necessary."

Robbins and Moore weren't the only IWW representatives on hand that day. Carlos Tresca spoke in Italian, repeating everything that Moore and Robbins had said, and Benjamin Schrager did the same in Polish. When Robbins did ask for a vote, everyone stood in agreement. Applause broke out, someone suggested they sing, and in one voice but a half-dozen different languages a rendition of "The Marsellaise" filled City Theatre. On Monday, January 6, the strikers, many of them anyway, would again become workers.

While Lunn was back in Schenectady during this time, there were Schenectady Socialists in Little Falls, reporting back to him on all the activity that was taking place. In his January 3 article, he took a few paragraphs to point out Schenectady's contribution to the fight.

"We believe no small share of the credit of winning the Little Falls strike belongs to the Socialist Party of this city," wrote Lunn. "Close on to $1,500 of money has been sent. Clothes and provisions have been supplied to the strikers. The strikers' children have been entertained by friends in Schenectady. Every Socialist of Schenectady who has had to go to jail because of his activities in this industrial war will feel that it has been worthwhile."

On Saturday, Jan. 4, Lunn paid a visit to the governor's office in Albany and found a very sympathetic ear in Sulzer. "I didn't know when I called on the governor," Lunn told the New York Press, "that I would find a willing witness for the defense in the case that is pending against me in Little Falls."

Sulzer evidently told Lunn that while he was campaigning for governor last fall he asked to be shown the precise spot where the mayor had been arrested for "inciting a riot among the striking workers." Sulzer then went to that location and began speaking to the striking workers only to be stopped by Chief Long. According to Sulzer's story, as told by Lunn, Sulzer didn't stop speaking and Long shouted at him, "I'd arrest you, too, if you weren't the Democratic candidate for governor. You've got the nerve of 30 brass monkeys."

Sulzer finished his stump speech without any more incident. The story was great news for Lunn, who said he probably wouldn't feel compelled to call Sulzer as a witness for the defense.

"Of course I do not think I should have to call on the governor to prove my innocence," Lunn told reporters. "Seriously speaking, however, I would like to say I feel confident no man will be deprived of the constitutional right of free speech in the time William Sulzer is in Albany."

When reporters asked Sulzer for his version of his conversation with Lunn he offered only this brief response.

"Yes, Mr. Lunn called on me and we had a chat," said Sulzer. "Whatever he has told you about our conversation is true."

On Jan. 11, Sulzer continued to demonstrate his support for Lunn when The New York Times reported that the Governor would be a witness on Lunn's behalf. In response to a reporter's question about being subpoenaed to testify in the case, Sulzer said, "I am a plain citizen, and will obey the mandate of the court." When the Times suggested that the governor was exempt from a subpoena, he replied, "I shall waive technicalities in the interest of due administration of the law." But, as Lunn had suggested a few days earlier, he never asked for Sulzer's help.

Back on Tuesday, January 7, Justice Andrews denied Lunn's request to inspect the minutes of the Herkimer County grand jury which had indicted him in December. According to the Rome Daily Sentinel and other press reports, Andrews was evidently not willing to create such a precedent. However, his statement for the record must have given Lunn hope. "It may well be doubted whether the evidence submitted by the committing magistrate would justify an indictment if unsupplemented," Andrews wrote.

Lunn's other attorney, Assistant Corporation Counsel James J. Barry, told reporters after getting the ruling by Andrews that his client would enter a demurrer to Judge Charles Bell on the grounds that "the facts stated in the indictment of the mayor on a charge of inciting to riot did not constitute a crime, and that the indictment contains matter that, if true, would constitute a legal justification or excuse for the acts charged."

Also on January 7, 1913, Lunn got a letter from a supporter in Little Falls. The short note arrived on stationary of the New York Central & Hudson River Railroad.

"It will probably interest you to know that the foreman of the grand jury was the superintendant of the local gas and electric company, who has boasted that he got back at you for reducing the price of gas in Schenectady," said the letter. "That is the combination you are up against. I think you will beat the bunch to a frazzle if you get the right kind of lawyer. It was the two local Catholic priests who inflamed Collins and Dusty against you after your arrest, but it was the city attorney who first told Chief Long to arrest you." The letter was signed, "Admirer."

The first few weeks in January were busy ones for Lunn. Along with all his issues relating to the Little Falls' situation, he was being criticized in the press again by his former business manager at The Citizen, Ben Henry. There was the continuing struggle over the bond issue for new parks, and there was a fight for control of the United People's Church between Lunn and his supporters and the congregation's old guard, that didn't appreciate the socialist incursion into their congregation. Lunn's trial in Herkimer was supposed to have begun in late January, but Judge Bell first had to rule on the demurrer filed by Cooper and Barry and he did that on January 20, informing the attorneys that their request had been denied. Cooper then asked for an immediate trial but was also rebuffed, Bell fixing the court date for Lunn's case for February 17.

In a speech Sunday morning, January 26 in Schenectady, Lunn talked about "Direct Action and Sabotage," and made a clean break from Haywood while also distancing himself from the IWW.

"William D. Haywood or any other man who advocates direct action, violence or sabotage ought to be expelled from the Socialist Party," said Lunn.

The Union Star reported that many IWW members were in the audience and one posed a question to Lunn: "Do you believe in the IWW?"

"From all I've been able to gain from observation and some little experience, the IWW is not so much an organization. It is rather a state of mind."

Lunn wasn't the only Socialist who thought Haywood too extreme. Big Bill was getting criticized from many corners, including Eugene Debs, and the in-fighting was quite discouraging for some, including Helen Keller.

"What, are we to put difference of party tactics before the desperate needs of the workers," said Keller. "It is with the deepest regret I have read the attacks upon Comrade Haywood which have appeared in the National Socialists. When will the champions of the oppressed unite, and thus hasten the day of deliverance?"

Judge Bell, meanwhile, kept himself busy over the first six months of 1913 dealing with the many different cases and appeals connected to the Little Falls strike. He didn't get to Lunn and Bakeman until July 17, and when he did the news was good for the two former ministers, with Bell reversing their convictions and allowing them to go free. No 50 days in jail and no $50 fine said Bell, citing the constitutional weakness of Section 145 of the Little Falls charter as the reason for his reversal. He did, however, feel compelled to offer a lecture, criticizing Lunn for his involvement in the Little Falls strike.

"My inclination would be to affirm the judgement appealed from, for it seems to me that it was very unbecoming for this defendant, mayor of the city of Schenectady, to go, incognito or otherwise, to the sister city of Little Falls, which then had all the trouble its mayor and officers could attend to, and attempt to do something that would bring them more trouble."

Bell finished up by referring back to Section 145 of the city charter. "The conclusion reached herein is, that the charter of the city of Little Falls contains no provision for the punishment of the acts enumerated in Section 145, and in that respect is nugatory, and there was no authority to impose said sentence. The judgment is, therefore, reversed."

Supporters of Lunn and Bakeman suggested the pair should file suit against the city of Little Falls. Bakeman, in his typical combative manner, told The Citizen, "I'm sorry that County Judge Bell reversed Recorder Collins' sentence. I'd love to have had the question taken to the highest courts in the country."

Lunn seemed content to see the issue end, and had no interest in taking any legal action.

"As my suit would go before Recorder Collins, I'm afraid it would do me no good for he has already ruled that my arrest was justifiable," said Lunn. "The funniest thing in the whole affair it seems to me is that part of Judge Bell's opinion in which he says clearly that I was guilty of no offense, yet he gives it as his personal inclination that I should be punished."

Lunn must have felt vindicated, and with the Little Falls chapter of his life behind him, he turned all of his focus back to Schenectady and his job as mayor. The summer of 1913 must have been a happy one for him. He could list among his many accomplishments the increase in minimum wage for city employees, from $1.75 to $2.25 for an eight-hour day; the creation of a garbage disposal plant and free garbage collection; and the construction of three new school buildings in the city and major additions and renovations to three others. He also won his battle for a new park system, although he did have to settle for a $300,000 price tag instead of his proposed $800,000 bond. To the park commission, which created Central Park, he appointed his fellow Socialist, Steinmetz; Hooper C. Ball, a Republican; Prof. Howard Opdyke, a Progressive; Harry A. Engle, a Democrat; and a female physician, Dr. Emma Wing-Thompson, who came on board with no political affiliation. The inclusion of just one Socialist on the park commission infuriated Socialists both at the local and state level.

The summer of 1913 also included another court case for Lunn. When the city was trying to install a new sewer pipe along Front Street, a small group of trees had to be cut down. But a property owner in the area got a court injunction stopping the work. Lunn, displaying a rarely-seen temper, marched down to Front Street and cut down the tree himself with an axe, arguing that he did it for the public good. He was fined $100 for contempt of court. This time, after an unsuccessful appeal, he paid the fine.

Lunn was also preparing for another election in the fall of 1913, and while there was a staunch group of anti-Lunnites in the Socialist local, the mayor did earn his party's nomination. But on election day, 1913, the voters of Schenectady put Lunn out of office, showing their preference for the fusion candidate, J. Teller Schoolcraft. An insurance agent and real estate salesman, Schoolcraft told the voters, "I solemnly promise you to place between me and all political gangs – past gangs, present gangs and future gangs – a gulf as deep and dark and broad as the everlasting gulf between God and socialism."

Schoolcraft got 9,222 votes to Lunn's 7,402. Lunn pointed out that his total vote count from the 1913 election was actually larger than what he received in 1911 – by 735 votes – so he and his supporters argued that socialism was actually growing in popularity in Schenectady and around the country. The Socialist ticket, however, also took a beating, losing its control of the city council and the county board of supervisors. The only Socialist victory came in the race for sheriff, and Herbert Merrill, the Socialist state assemblyman from Schenectady, lost his bid for re-election.

The enthusiasm with which both city newspapers supported the election of Schoolcraft wasn't restricted to the editorial page. The Union Star reminded its readers with a large front page story how what it perceived as Lunn's lack of regard for law and order led to the death of 11-year-old Gladys Dwyer the winter before. "There is a mute reminder in the cemetery, the grave of the girl who was killed when he suspended the anti-coasting ordinance, an illegal act on his part." The Gazette, meanwhile, was just as consistently vitriolic as its competitor, arguing that a vote for Lunn or any socialist was a vote for "Godlessness," echoing Schoolcraft's words. "Do you believe in Socialism or Americanism, the Red Flag or the American Flag?"

In Wednesday's Gazette following his election, Schoolcraft repeated a talking point about socialism's threat to business interests repeated throughout September and October of 1913 by Democrats and Republicans. "The citizens of the city have shown that they do not approve of the past two years of Socialism, with its uncertainties, and the fear and suspicion with which the business world has looked upon Schenectady," said the new mayor. "They have shown they desire the credit and good name of Old Dorp to be placed upon a plane commensurate with its greatness."

Lunn certainly had a different viewpoint of socialism's impact on the city, and on December 30, 1913, a Tuesday night, he delivered his final message to its citizens at a special meeting of the Common Council.

"When the present Socialist administration was elected to office grave fears were expressed as to the effect it would have on the credit and prosperity of the city," Lunn began. "It was freely prophesied that the great industrial plants would adopt a policy of retrenchment with the result that Schenectady would suffer two years of hardship due to thousands being unemployed. Instead of this direful prophecy coming true just the opposite has actually occurred. The past two years register the high water mark of prosperity for the city."

Lunn pointed out that more men were employed at GE and ALCO during his time as mayor than ever before, and as for city employees their wages had increased from $1.75 to $2.25 for an eight-hour day. Lunn also pointed out many public improvements, including the free collection of garbage which had begun earlier in 1913. The garbage disposal plant to handle that waste would begin operating in 1914, and there were also improvements to the city's sewage system aimed at providing healthier drinking water while also cleaning up the Mohawk River.

"We have one of the most beautiful rivers in the country," said Lunn. "The beautiful Mohawk should be restored to the condition when it can be called the healthful Mohawk River. This cannot be done until the sewage of a great city ceases to contaminate its waters."

Lunn went on to talk about renovations to three of the city's school buildings and plans to construct three more. There were parks and playgrounds that had been agreed upon and would be built, and Lunn also noted how 850 "outside privy vaults" had been eliminated within city limits and only a few remained. His administration had also reduced the cost of paving roads and overseen improvements to the Cotton Factory Hollow Bridge, better linking the Ninth Ward's 15,000 residents to the rest of the city. Lunn also established a City Planning Commission, designed to be a non-partisan group which should "have the confidence of the vast majority of people of our city."

In November of 1913, after losing the mayoral office to Schoolcraft, Lunn had his own strike to deal with when nearly 15,000 GE workers walked off the job. A lame duck leader at this point, Lunn came out in support of the strikers, and appointed 30 of the workers to act as special deputies and patrol the picket lines. He also said none of the strikers will go hungry while he's mayor, and served as a mediator between GE President G.E. Emmons and the workers, negotiating a favorable end to the strike for the workers within five days.

Despite losing the mayor's office, Lunn must have felt somewhat optimistic about his political future and the path ahead for socialism. In truth, Lunn's career was far from over, but the political ideology to which he had attached himself was indeed on the decline. As history tells us, 1912 was socialism's high water mark in the U.S., and as membership in the party decreased, Lunn's strong socialist connections, even after his switch to the Democratic party, kept him from playing too significant a role in any larger political arena. Yes, along with three more terms as mayor, he was elected to the U.S. Congress for two years and joined Al Smith in Albany as Lieutenant Governor, another two-year term. He was also a popular choice among fellow Democrats to succeed Smith as governor of New York, but as bright as his prospects may have seemed to some, it wasn't to be. As America came out of the great World War and looked ahead to the 1920s, the idea of a one-time devout Socialist carrying too much political clout was becoming less and less viable. Also, as Lunn's star was fading in the 1920s, New York politics would be dominated by two of the state's most magnetic and powerful men ever, Franklin D. Roosevelt and Al Smith.

CHAPTER 23

Leaving Socialism

In July 1940, two years away from retirement as New York's Public Service Commissioner, Lunn sat down with a reporter from the Albany Knickerbocker News and reflected on his long political career.

"It amuses me that looking back to 1912 when I was mayor of Schenectady and charged then with being a radical Socialist, that those things I advocated and attempted to incorporate in government are now accepted and looked upon as conservative policies."

Lunn had flirted with the Republican Party early in his life and become a staunch Socialist for half a decade before firmly entrenching himself with the Democrats. As a result he was often accused of flip-flopping and being guilty of political expediency by the city's two major newspapers. Even The Citizen, once his own powerful voice, ran a large cartoon of Lunn as a chameleon in 1918 with the caption, "Georgie's Changing Political Hue, Where Will He Light Next?"

Lunn did recover from his 1913 defeat for mayor. Despite constant bickering inside the Schenectady Socialist local, he regained the mayoral seat in 1915 and helped Steinmetz win election as President of the City Council. They were helped when the Democrats, Republicans and Progressives could no longer maintain the partnership that had helped them win in 1913. Lunn had 6,069 votes, while former mayor Horace Van Voast, a Republican, picked up 5,041 votes. Democrat Henry Buhrmaster was next with 3,435 votes, while the local Progressives had become irrelevant by then and failed to nominate a candidate.

But while Lunn and Steinmetz both enjoyed a triumphant return to office in 1915, the Socialists did lose control of the city council when only two members of the party retained their seats.

On November 22, soon after getting a telegram of congratulations from Eugene Debs, Lunn wrote back to Debs, indicating he and Steinmetz would remain strong advocates for socialism.

"Steinie and myself as well as all other Socialists to be associated with us in the coming administration will do everything in our power to give such service as will make the mass of people realize that the great big meaning of socialism is above all service to the people," wrote Lunn. "Trusting that I will be able to welcome you here during my term as mayor I remain, sincerely your comrade, George R. Lunn."

But the party squabbles got worse early in Lunn's second term, again mostly over his appointments of non-Socialists to important positions in the administration. In February, the Socialist local determined that Lunn had violated the party's state constitution regarding appointments – Lunn plead guilty – but did not gain the two-thirds majority to expel the mayor from the party. The state committee took over, dealing with Lunn by revoking the local's charter.

Steinmetz wasted little time showing he still supported Lunn, sending a statement to the Gazette which the newspaper ran on February 11, 1916.

"It is ridiculous to assume that a self-constituted body of less than two hundred, usually less than one hundred men, as the Schenectady local, could sit in judgment and reverse the action of more than 6,000 Socialist voters, who a few weeks ago expressed their view who should represent them in the administration of the city... While in some European countries as Germany, there seems to be an approach between socialism and autocratic monarchy, here in America we certainly are not prepared to abandon democracy and surrender our party government to the dictation of an irresponsible autocracy, a self constituted party machine."

Steinmetz went on to call the Socialist local "inefficient and antiquated," and urged it to "drop all the unessential features.... which have nothing to do with socialism."

Despite Steinmetz's support, Lunn was out of the Socialist party in March. Before the party primary in April, Lunn put up

one more fight, trying to reclaim control of the local at an informal meeting at Steinmetz's house. But, when members of the
anti-Lunn faction showed up, a brawl nearly broke out according to the Gazette's account on April 12. Back in January, Lunn
had also resigned from his position as editor of The Citizen, and
in June he lost control of the newspaper at the annual stockhold-
ers meeting. Lunn was suddenly a mayor without a party and his
major propaganda tool.

As the months wore on in 1916, Lunn's working relationship
with Steinmetz began to fracture and their friendship became
strained. While Lunn remained independent politically for a
short time, he did accept the Democratic endorsement to run
for Congress, and also attached himself to President Wilson's re-
election bid. Steinmetz, meanwhile, was supporting former New
York governor and Glens Falls native Charles Evans Hughes, a
Republican, for president. Steinmetz argued for U.S. neutral-
ity in the World War across the Atlantic, while Lunn, backing
Wilson, eventually resigned himself to the fact that war would
come. When the U.S. did get involved, Steinmetz made the decision in early 1918 to join the war effort and help the U.S. Navy
develop shells that would explode a few feet before hitting the
ground, making them much more efficient. Lunn, having been
elected to Congress and been placed on the Committee of Military Affairs, helped Steinmetz get an appointment to the Inven-
tions Section of the War Department in May of 1918. The same
war that had come between them helped mend their relationship, and when Steinmetz died in October of 1923 at the age of
58, Lunn was one of the pall bearers at his funeral.

While Lunn supported Wilson because he had kept the U.S.
out of the European conflict, both men eventually changed
their minds, in large part due to Germany's refusal to cease its
unbridled U-boat attacks. Wilson ended up edging Hughes, the
former New York governor, by 23 electoral votes in the presidential race, while Lunn, getting endorsed by the Democrats,
Progressives, Independent and American parties, defeated Re-

publican Henry DeForest by approximately 500 votes to earn the right to represent Schenectady, Montgomery, Fulton and Hamilton counties in Washington, D.C.

Lunn's victory was improbable. While he may have been a popular vote-getter, there were 13,400 registered Republicans in Schenectady County and only 6,441 Democrats, and DeForest was a popular former Republican congressman from Schenectady. Lunn, however, collected 10,131 votes in the county and DeForest had 7,437. The Socialists, meanwhile, with a registration of 1,101 voters, ran Merrill for Congress and the former state assemblyman finished a distant third with 1,566 votes.

While their campaign speeches may have been filled with anti-war rhetoric, Wilson and Lunn were soon singing another tune. On April 2, 1917, Wilson asked Congress to declare war on Germany, and Lunn concurred, offering his reasons in an impassioned speech before Congress on April 5.

"Mr. Chairman, after eight years in which I have gone up and down this country talking against war, being opposed to war under any form or for any reason, when after that position a man can come to the place where he is willing to admit that there are occasions when war is the only arbitrament and makes that decision, it is time to vote against this resolution. I say that it would be easier for me a thousand times to vote no than to vote aye.

"But Mr. Chairman, we are facing the greatest national crisis in our history, and we have only two ways open to us. One is to accept a war, thrust upon us by the repeated aggressions of a power which recognizes no law but its own imperial will. The other is to defeat the resolution and adopt the policy of absolute submission. The latter course to my mind is unthinkable. I will vote aye for this resolution, but I do so with a heavy heart, a saddened soul. I, too, have hoped for peace, prayed for peace, but I can not be of the number who cry, 'peace, peace,'" when there is no hope."

CHAPTER 24

Al Smith and FDR

1918 must have seemed like an exciting time for Lunn. He was a member of Congress in one of the two major political parties, and he was growing nearer and nearer to Wilson's inner circle. The president had proposed his post-war plan for Europe with his 14 Points speech, much of it written by Lippman, back on January 8, 1918, and Lunn had argued long and hard in favor of Wilson's world view. In November, however, Lunn failed to win re-election to Congress, losing to Schenectady dentist Frank Crowther, who would hold onto that seat for 24 years. A week later the war was over, but between the election and March 3, 1919 when his term as Congressman would expire, Lunn remained patiently in Washington, D.C., waiting for an appointment to a diplomatic post or to play a huge role in helping Wilson sell the League of Nations. None of those things materialized.

In May of 1949, a few months after Lunn's death, Willliam Efner, then the Schenectady City Historian, offered his take on Lunn's disappointing winter of 1918-19 in a letter to Rev. William N.P. Daily of Amsterdam.

"I saw Lunn topple from a place of prime importance in the Wilson administration to a man in search of a job," wrote Efner, who had left his life as a Schenectady reporter behind and accompanied Lunn to Washington where the new Congressman helped him land a position as an efficiency expert in the War Department. According to Efner, both he and Lunn were to play major roles in a new organization designed to "perpetuate Wilson's 14 Points."

"Assistant Secretary of the Treasury, [Thomas] Love, my big boss," wrote Efner, "then suggested that I be put in charge of the work of organization; agreeing that Lunn should be director. I was to have the Washington office; Lunn the national field. He was to continually travel. He was to address college bodies, educational institutes, conventions, church gatherings – whenever men and women gathered. He was to be the apostle of the Wilsonian social and economic theories."

All these plans, according to Efner, were being made by Secretary of War Newton D. Baker while Wilson was at the Paris Peace Talks during the first half of 1919. When the president got back to Washington, "he turned a deaf ear to the wishes of practically his entire cabinet and the leaders of Congress. The 'great adventure' folded up over night. Both Lunn and I were without jobs we thought we had for a certainty."

How accurate the details of Efner's story are we don't know, but it seems he and Lunn were genuinely surprised and devastated by events between November of 1918 and June of 1919.

"One night we walked the streets until a very late hour," Efner continued in his letter to Daly, who had written suggesting the City Historian write a biography of Lunn. "He was broken in spirit. He unburdened himself. He did not want to leave Washington. He could not understand why Wilson would not give him a post in a foreign country – his ambition. He talked of a possible return to the pulpit; spoke of his powers over the masses; referred to his evangelistic experiences. Then, he came back to Schenectady."

There had been talk of Lunn being groomed for the governor's office as early as 1916, and in the summer of 1918, before he lost re-election to the Congress, the talk got serious. On a hot Monday afternoon, July 5, a group of Democrats from Schenectady, Montgomery, Fulton and Hamilton counties met at the Hotel Barnes in Amsterdam and determined that their representative to Congress would make a great governor. The group of 36 powerful Democrats, including a former nemesis of Lunn's, Gazette publisher Gerardus Smith, overwhelmingly decided to ask Lunn to run for the state's highest office. Lunn began his response the next day at the Mohawk Hotel in Schenectady by saying he was very happy being a member of the U.S. House of Representatives.

"However, the nomination for governor of the Empire State, with its opportunity for service, is an honor conferred upon but few men, and while my personal wish is to be returned to Washington, if your judgment appears to be confirmed by the Democrats generally, I will enter the race, determined that the Democratic Party shall win."

The resolution the group had presented Lunn was quite complimentary.

"Throughout his public career, as mayor of the city of Schenectady, as representative in the greatest law-making body in the world, he has displayed keen and farseeing statesmanship," offered the Democratic leaders. "Representative Lunn has shown how well he can meet the demands of war. At the same time, he has a full realization of the most effective part which those remaining at home must play in aiding our soldiers and sailors on battlefield and on sea. He has taken a leading part in championing the effective war-measures of the national administration presided over by President Woodrow Wilson. His quick perception and wonderful tact in dealing with all the trying problems of national life in these tragic times stamp him as one of the leading and most valuable supporters of our illustrious president."

The resolution went on to mention Lunn's role in helping Wilson form U.S. war policy, and cited his "fearlessness and courage" for supporting women's suffrage regardless of the political consequences.

As it turned out, the political bosses in New York City had their own man in mind, Al Smith, and it was the Tammany Hall-backed candidate that became the Democratic choice and then the state's first Catholic governor, winning a two-year term from 1919-1921.

While Lunn probably wasn't too upset over losing the nomination to Smith in 1918, his defeat at the hands of Crowther was indeed a personal blow that struck deeply. It was a very close contest, and by Wednesday, November 6, the day after the election, Crowther could claim a 543-vote lead. Lunn's camp, however, wasn't conceding. Frank Cooper was still Lunn's legal counsel and argued that there were irregularities in the Gloversville vote, and that the soldier's absentee vote, when counted, would give Lunn the victory. There were nearly 2,000 ballots that wouldn't be counted until December 17, and with 75 percent of them going for Lunn – that was Cooper's guess – and with Lunn picking up more votes in Gloversville, the election could swing the other way.

There were numerous recounts over the next month, and while Lunn did pick up 35 more votes in Amsterdam, Crowther, a Liverpool, England native who moved to the U.S. when he was 3, was much more popular than anyone expected with the soldiers. On December 21, Cooper conceded to Supreme Court Justice H.C. Whitmyer that the fight was over. A graduate of Harvard Dental School and now 48, Crowther actually increased his margin of victory after a month of maneuvering by Lunn's lieutenants, finishing with a 637-vote cushion.

On February 5, 1919, nearly a month before his term would expire, Lunn hosted Crowther for breakfast at his Washington D.C. apartment. The new congressman was in the nation's capital for a meeting with other first-time representatives, and he remained in the U.S. House of Representatives until 1943 when, at the age of 72, he decided not to run for a 12th term. Crowther, who had moved to Schenectady in 1912, retired and moved to Pueblo, Colorado where he played the violin, painted landscapes and was a public speaker. He died in 1955 at the age of 85.

Lunn had convincingly carried the city of Schenectady against Crowther, and in November 1919 those voters put him back in the mayor's chair. Lunn defeated incumbent Republican Charles Simon, collecting 11,801 votes to 10,273 for Simon. Noonan was put up by the Socialist local and received 2,633 votes. Schenectadian voters proved quite progressive in 1918, also electing Rose Perkins Hale (Mrs. Edward Everett Hale Jr.) as a county supervisor in the Second Ward where she defeated Republican County Chairman Edwin Conde by two votes, 953-951. Also, Schenectady physician Dr. Elizabeth Gillette became the first women outside of New York City to win a seat in the New York Assembly. Both women were Democrats and Lunn supporters.

A few weeks after once again moving into his City Hall office, Lunn went to Albany on January 28 to testify at the State Capitol regarding the expulsion of five Socialists from the State Assembly. The five men, all duly- elected by their constituents, were deemed unfit for their office on January 7 by Assembly Speaker Thaddeus Sweet of Oswego. Citing their ties to the Socialist Party of America, "a disloyal organization composed exclusively of perpetual traitors," according to Sweet, New York's governing body voted, 140-6 with one abstention, to refuse to allow the five to take their seats in the chamber. Former governor Charles Evan Hughes and the current occupant of New York's highest office, Al Smith, both protested the ouster, but with Sweet quickly pushing things along, the voices of 60,000 Americans who had legally elected their representatives were ignored.

During Lunn's testimony at a January 28th hearing, the former Socialist told his story about the visit he received from Hunt and Noonan on election eve, 1911, regarding the resignation form the local would hold over his head during his first two years as mayor. Lunn painted what he felt was a truthful picture of the Schenectady local, and while his testimony wasn't necessarily helpful to the five Socialists - Samuel A. DeWitt, Samuel Orr, Charles Solomon, August Claessens and Louis Waldman – he made it clear he was not in support of disenfranchising 60,000 voters. When Seymour Stedman, an attorney for the five Socialists and Debs' 1920 running mate, asked Lunn for his opinion about the ongoing proceedings he responded by saying he was "very much opposed to it," even though "my antagonism for the Socialist Party is very great." On April 1, after debating the topic for 24 hours, the Assembly voted again and decided to expel Waldman, Claessens and Solomon, 116-28, and DeWitt and Orr, 104-40. When a special election was held in September to fill those seats, the five men all won re-election. This time around, the Assembly ousted Waldman, Claessens and Solomon and allowed Orr and DeWitt to take their seats. The two men, however, decided to resign in solidarity with the other three, and it wasn't until April of 1921 that the Assembly reversed itself. Without exception all five men went on to long and successful careers in either business or the legal system, and were universally held in high esteem.

Later in 1921, some upstate Democrats put up Lunn's name for the U.S. Senate, but Binghamton's Harry C. Walker won the primary. Lunn blamed the setback on all the disfavor he had sown over the years with the Tammany Hall party bosses in New York City. But in the fall of 1921 he was back in the winner's circle, earning a fourth term as mayor, defeating Republican Leon Dibble by nearly 3,000 votes, 12,846 to 10,147. John C. Bellingham was the Socialist pick and finished a distant third with 2,865 votes.

Then in 1922, Al Smith, who had lost his re-election bid for Governor in 1920, picked Lunn as his running mate and the pair were elected, taking over in Albany in January of 1923. By this time, Lunn had let up his relentless attacks on Tammany Hall, and was evidently deemed appropriate enough by city boss Charles F. Murphy and his cronies to become the Lieutenant Governor.

It was while campaigning for Lieutenant Governor that Lunn found himself being better received by Tammany Hall, due mostly to his popularity as a public speaker. He became one of the party's best spokesman throughout the state and New York City, giving rousing speeches at mass meetings in Manhattan, The Bronx, Queens and Kings County all in one night according to a report by the New York Evening Post.

The newspaper's reporter, Hans J. Adamson, even reported that Lunn might be "ready to loop his lariat around the vice-presidential nomination should the national standard bearer be a man from the South or West. On the other hand, Lieutenant Governor Lunn, who is somewhat ambidextrous, stands ready to lasso the gubernatorial nomination in the event governor Smith should be picked for national honors."

Adamson's prognosis wasn't quite spot on. Lunn was Smith's right-hand man for two years, but then lost his re-election bid in 1924 to a Republican, Seymour Lowman. Smith had won his third term, but at the time governors and their lieutenants had distinct and separate voting tallies. Lowman, who became Assistant Secretary of the Treasury in the Hoover Administration, was the last politician in New York independently elected lieutenant governor as his party's gubernatorial candidate was losing his bid at the state's highest office.

In 1925, Smith appointed Lunn as Public Service Commissioner, a post he would be reappointed to by Roosevelt and Herbert Lehman. The position had been created in 1907 to serve as a watchdog for the public trust, dealing with various state utilities and transportation issues. Lunn was perfect for the job, and spent 17 years at it. Some suggested Democratic Party officials liked seeing him busy with the Public Service Commission since it meant the popular politician/former Socialist wouldn't likely be seeking higher office. But once again, in 1928, enough Democrats thought him still enough of a viable candidate that he should run for governor. Edged by Smith for the Democratic nod in 1918, Lunn allowed his name to be placed in nomination at the 1928 state convention, thinking that FDR was going to play by the same rules. But what was supposed to be an "open" convention was actually being choreographed by FDR's handlers, and the Hyde Park native and former assistant Secretary of the Navy became the party's pick four years before being elected to lead the country.

In his letter to Daily a full two decades later, Efner once again told of Lunn's disappointment and his bitterness toward Roosevelt for pre-empting the normal nominating process. "He told me much concerning his dealings with Al Smith and Roosevelt and politics in general," wrote Efner, referring to a 1930 meeting with Lunn in Albany. "It was a sad story."

Efner also wrote of "the hatred that lay deep in Lunn's heart," for Roosevelt, but years later Schenectady historian Larry Hart suggested Efner was overstating the case, noting Lunn's support for the president throughout his three-plus terms as president. The two men, Lunn and FDR, did have an occasional correspondence throughout the 1930s, and on January 10, 1940 Lunn tele-graphed congratulations to Roosevelt as FDR began his third term as president. The chief executive wired back his thanks to Lunn later that day, extending his "warm best wishes."

CHAPTER 25

Epilogue

"The masters stand at the head of things;
They are lords of work and pay;
And we must run till the set of sun,
Because the masters say;
For we, for we are the underlings,
And the lords of bread are they;
And we must eat though they screw and cheat,
And when they nod, obey.

Philip Green Wright,
"The Cry of the Underlings," 1906.

George Lunn spent much of his life trying to right the inherent failings of capitalism, in particular the battle, as he saw it, between the one percent and the 99 percent. When he left elective politics, the fight did not stop. His long career as the state's Public Service Commissioner offered plenty of opportunities to continue that fight for the average worker and citizen, and it also kept Lunn out of the political arena, making room for other prominent Democrats with lofty aspirations.

For some, the enticing annual salary of $15,000 for Public Service Commissioner was a way for the party hierarchy to keep Lunn happy and out of the way. In an April 1942 editorial after his retirement, the Schenectady Gazette applauded Lunn's long public life and offered this take on his appointment to the Pulbic Service Commission, a decision which effectively ended his political career.

"He was too dangerous to the bosses to remain in circulation and was too difficult to control."

Lunn lived on Stratford Road in the GE Realty Plot in Schenectady until 1932. He had lost his wife, Mabel, to a heart attack the year before in October 1931. On November 4, 1932, he remarried, exchanging vows in Brooklyn with Anita Jensen Oliver, a widow from California. The couple had met earlier in the year at a dinner party at Lunn's sister's home in Oakland. Jensen had been married to a successful engineer and was well known in the Bay area as a social activist. It was also during this time, 1931-32, that Lunn was Commander-in-Chief of the United Spanish War Veterans. And while he was out of elective politics, he continued to serve as a delegate to the Democratic National Convention.

While he kept a legal residence in Schenectady for a few years, Lunn and his new wife lived in Albany and then moved to Selkirk in 1938. They spent much of their time in California near San Diego after he retired from the state, but were regular visitors to upstate New York and often summered in Newfane, Vermont with different members of Lunn's family.

When he retired as Public Service Commissioner, Governor Lehman wrote a letter to Lunn thanking him for his service. Part of the letter was published in the Gazette.

"May I take this opportunity of thanking you for the splendid service which you have rendered to the people of the state not only as a public service commissioner but in many other important public positions over a period of more than a quarter of a century," said Lehman. "As mayor of Schenectady, as lieutenant governor of the state and as public service commissioner you always have been zealous in the public interest and you have served with fidelity and devotion. On behalf of your fellow citizens, please accept my very sincere thanks."

Lunn died at the age of 75 on November 27, 1948, leaving behind his spouse and five children (three daughters and two sons) from his first marriage. Lunn, who was also survived by a brother and two sisters, was buried in Forest Lawn Park Cemetery in Glendale, California. Anita, nine years younger than Lunn, died in 1975 at the age of 93.

* * *

On November 29, 1948 the Schenectady City Council adopted Resolution No. 2176, directing all the flags on city buildings be lowered to half mast in Lunn's honor. The resolution, offered by Councilman Arthur Hilliard, a Democrat, said in part, "Due to his ever pleasant smile, genial personality and charm, he endeared himself to those who had the good fortune of knowing him, and, due to his progressiveness, his foresight, his industry, his courage, integrity and fairness, he earned the respect and admiration of not only the people of Schenectady, but the people of the great state of New York as well." The resolution passed unanimously with the endorsement of Mayor Owen Begley.

Efner always argued that Lunn "was an honest-to-goodness reformer but never a Socialist at heart." But that assessment comes from someone who regarded himself as a "very close friend." Efner may have been trying to protect Lunn's legacy as well as explain why someone with his political acumen failed to reach greater heights.

However you summarize the man, he was undoubtedly a fine politician and a popular vote-getter whose integrity and personal morality trumped any political allegiance he might have. Former city and county historian Larry Hart (1920-2004) knew Lunn and remembered how his popularity seemed to transcend politics. "My parents were staunch Republicans, but they loved Lunn," he said.

To his friends and family members, Lunn was revered. In November 2003, 92-year-old Maxine Lunn, who married Lunn's youngest son Raymond, told the Gazette that Lunn "was a very sweet and affectionate person. He wasn't at all cold or formal with us. I ended up feeling pretty close to him, and he'd always put his arms around you and give you a hug. He really was the nicest man."

Bennison, Patrick C., "The Red Phoenix 1912 Textile Strike," master's thesis at Boston College, 1986.

Common Council Minutes, City of Schenectady, 1911-1913, 1948

Cooke, Alistaire, "The Vintage Mencken," Alfred A. Knopf and Random House, New York, 1955.

Cooney, Michael, "The Red Nurse: A Story of the Little Falls Textile Strike of 1912," Wilderness Hill Books, 2012, Valatie, N.Y.

Dubofsky, Melvin, "Big Bill Haywood," St. Martin's Press, New York, 1987.

Eveson, Phiip, "The 1904-1905 Welsh Revival," Grace Magazine, Quinta Press, Shropshire, England, 2010.

Freeberg, Ernest, "Democracy's Prisoner: Eugene V. Debs, The Great War, and the Right to Dissent," Harvard University Press, Cambridge, Mass., 2010.

Gaffield, Chad "Big Business: The Working Class and Socialism in Schenectady, 1911-1916."

Gardner, George, "The Schenectadians: The Story of Schenectady's 20th Century and the Men Who Helped Shape It," iUniverse, 2001.

Hart, Larry, "Schenectady's Golden Era 1880-1930," Old Dorp Books, Scotia, 1974.

Hendrickson, Kenneth, "George R. Lunn and the Socialist Era in Schenectady, New York, 1909-1916." New York History, Volume 47, No. 1, January 1966.

Graham, Frank, "Al Smith American: An Informal Biography," G.P. Putnam's Sons, New York, 1945.

Klatnick, Arnold, "Socialist Municipal Administrations in Four American Cities: Milwaukee, Schenectady, New Castle, Pennsylvania, and Conneaut, Ohio, 1910-1916." 1982 PhD thesis for New York University.

Kline, Ronald R., "Steinmetz: Engineer and Socialist," The Century Company, New York, 1992.

Lunn, George, "Features of the Schenectady Revival," Homiletic Review, Volume 49, March 1905.

MacAdam, George, "Where Socialism Failed Miserably," New York Times.

McMartin, Joseph A, "Labor's Great War: The Struggle for Industrial Democracy and the Origins of Modern American Labor Relations, 1912-1921."

Messer-Kruse, Timothy, "The Trial of the Haymarket Anarchists: Terrorism and Justice in the Gilded Age," Palgrave-Macmillan, New York, 2011.

Miller, Douglas K, "Socialism Rule in Schenectady Ends," Schenectady Gazette, Jan. 3, 1920.

Pascussi, Robert R., "Electric City Immigrants: Italians and Poles of Schenectady, N.Y., 1880-1930," State University of New York at Albany, Department of History, 1984.

Pontius, K.S., DeJohn, G.F. and Dykstra, J.D., "3 Centuries: The History of the First Reformed Church of Schenectady, 1680-1980, published by FRC of Schenectady, 1980.

Rabinowitz, Matilda, "Immigrant Girl, Radial Woman: A Memoir from the Early 20th Century, Cornell University Press, 2017.

Radford, Gail, "The Rise of the Public Authority in State Building and Economic Development in Twentieth Century America." University of Chicago Press, July 2013.

Reynolds, Cuyler, "Hudson-Mohawk Genealogical and Family Memoirs," Lewis Historical Publishing Company, New York, 1911.

Rich, Kathryn, "George R. Lunn: Socialist Mayor of Schenectady," Schenectady County Public Library, 1966.

Riordan, William, "Plunkitt of Tammany Hall," E.P. Dutton and Company, New York, 1963.

Snyder, Robert E., "Women, Wobblies and Workers' Rights: The 1912 Textile Strike in Little Falls, New York History Journal, Fenimore Art Museum, Cooperstown, 1979.

Steel, Ronald, "Walter Lippmann and the American Century." Little, Brown and Company, New York, 1980.

Tussey, Jenny, "Eugene V. Debs Speaks," Pathfinder Press, New York, 1970.

Urofsky, Melvin I., "A Note on the Expulsion of the Five Socialists," New York History, Volume 47, No. 1, 1966.

Primary Newspapers

Schenectady Gazette, Schenectady Union Star, The Citizen, Albany Times Union, Albany Knickerbocker Press, New York Times, Little Falls Evening Times.

Other Newspapers

Altamont Enterprise, Brooklyn Eagle, Common Cause, Denver Post, Little Falls Journal and Courier, New York Call, New York Evening Post, New York Sun, Rome Daily Sentinel, Syracuse Post Standard, Syracuse Herald, Utica Globe, Utica Observer-Dispatch.

INDEX

G

Garbage, 70.

Garfield, James, 11.

Garrick Theater (Chicago), 156.

General Electric, 35, 39, 56, 58-59, 61, 77, 121, 143, 146, 165, 173, 182.

General Electric Realty Plot, 79, 198.

Gilbert, Judson, 122, 171.

Gilbert, Knitting Mill (Little Falls), 123.

Gilded Age, 7.

Gillette, Chester, 140.

Gillette, Dr. Elizabeth, 192.

Gilpatrick Hotel (Milwaukee), 141.

Giovannitti, Arturo, 75-76.

Glens Falls, 50.

Glenn's Hotel and Restaurant, 62.

Gloversville, 38, 52, 116, 192.

Goldman, Emma, 36-40.

Gompers, Samuel, 154.

Goose Hill, 60.

Gospel Tent Evangel, 25.

Gould, Henry, 78.

Great Chicago Fire, 27.

Greene, James, A., 172.

Gregg, Rev. David, 42.

Griffis, William Elliot, 15-16.

G.R. Lunn and Associates, 101-102, 167.

H

Hale Jr, Edward Everett, 119, 142-145.

Hale, Edward Everett, 119.

Hale, Rose Perkins, 73, 192.

Haley, Michael, 136-138.

Hanford, Benjamin, 29-30.

Harding, Warren G., 31.

Harlem Socialist Club, 123.

Harrrison, Abram, 52.

Hart, Larry, 195, 199.

Harvard, 68, 76, 87-88, 91, 96.

Harvard Advocate, 91.

Harvard Lampoon, 91.

Harvard Socialist Club, 74, 85.

Hathaway, William, 56.

Haymarket Riot of 1886, 36, 38.

Haywood, Big Bill, 28-30, 123, 137, 140, 150, 153, 173, 178-179.

Healy, Mabel, 14.

Hearst, William Randolph, 34.

Henry, Ben S., 53, 116-117, 178.

Herkimer County Jail, 128, 149.

Herkimer, Gen. Nicholas, 130.

Herron, William, 56, 58-59, 61, 63.

Hickey, Jim, 167-168.

Hilliard, Arthur, 199.

Hillquist, Morris, 67, 72, 86-87, 100, 112, 116.

Hippodrome Theater (Little Falls), 150.

Hirsch, Fred, 128, 152.

Hoan, Daniel, 84.

Hoffman, Frank S., 17.

Hoffmans, 73.

Holy Trinity Church (Brooklyn), 64.

Home Rule, 74.

Homestead Strike, 37.

Hooker, James, 58-59.

Hoover, Herbert, 195.

Hornaday, Dr. N.S., 11.

Hotel Barney (Amsterdam), 190.

Hudson River, 13.

Hughes, Gov. Charles Evans, 34, 50, 187, 193.

Humphrey Detective Agency, 135-136, 138, 160.

Humphrey, William A., 139.

Hunt, Russell, 60, 68, 82, 111-112, 114, 193.

Hurley, Richard, 164.

115, 124, 160, 167-168, 173, 176, 180, 185-186.

Socialist Party of America, 28, 46-47, 58, 147, 153.

Sokol Hall (Little Falls), 137, 151, 155-156.

Solomon, Charles, 193.

Sons and Daughters of Washington, 52.

Spanish-American War, 13, 17, 68.

Special Investigative Committee, 60.

Springborn, William J., 155-156.

St. George's Episcopal Church, 81.

St. John the Evangelist, 24.

Stanford, Bertha (Sanford), 19-24.

Stanford, Charles, 23.

Stanford, Grant 23.

Stanford, Leland, 23.

Stanford, Welton 23-24.

Stanton, Kathleen, 16.

State Board of Mediation, 170.

State Conservation Commission, 50.

State Street Methodist Episcopal Church (First United Methodist), 19-21, 23, 41, 63.

Stedman, Seymour, 193.

Steel, Ronald, 85-86.

Steffins, Lincoln, 33-34, 49, 85.

Steinmetz, Charles Proteus, 77-79, 161-162, 180, 185-187.

Stern, Max., 98.

Stokes, Helen, 64, 67, 111.

Stoller, James, 44.

Stratford, Road, 198.

Strebel, Gustav, 99.

Sullivan, Anne, 91-93, 95-96.

Sulzer, Gov. William, 52, 172, 176-177.

Sweeney, Daniel J., 102, 114.

Sweet, Thaddeus, 193.

Swinton, John, 31.

Swiss Federal Polytechnic Institute, 78.

Syndicalism, 38.

Syracuse, 9.

Syracuse Herald, 127.

Syracuse Journal, 172.

T

Taft, William Howard, 34, 50, 65, 73, 83, 141, 147.

Tammany Hall, 49, 88, 191, 194.

Tarbell, Ida, 33.

Taylor, Rev. Dr., 81.

Terre Haute, Indiana, 30-31.

Tesla, Nicola, 77.

Thomas, Herkimer attorney, 163-164.

Thomson-Houston Electrical Company, 43.

Thorne, Jennie May, 165-167.

Tresca, Carlos, 176.

Triangle Shirtwait Factory Fire, 50, 122.

Trinity Reformed Church (Amsterdam), 64.

Turnbull, William, 97.

Twilight Club (New York City), 64.

U

Union College, 15, 25, 55, 78, 89.

Union Theological Seminary, 13, 16.

United People's Church, 50, 63, 72, 116, 133, 142, 153, 166, 178.

United Textile Workers, 154.

University Club (Syracuse), 64.

University of Breslau, 77.

U.S. Spanish-American War Veterans, 198.

USS Battleship Maine, 13.
Utica, 9, 38, 98, 133, 137-138, 142, 153.
Utica Daily Observer, 45.
Utica Observer Dispatch, 171-172.
Utica Globe, 60.

V

Vale Cemetery, 98.
Van Curler Arent, 8.
Van Curler Theatre, 51.
Van Rensselaer, Stephen, 8.
Van Vechten, Hawley, 53, 67, 115-116.
Van Voast, Horace, 38, 185.
Van Voast, John, 43.
Van Vorst, James, 92.
Van Vorst, Mary, 92.
Vaughn, George, 149, 152.
Vermilyea, Ashbel, 15.
Vietnam War, 85, 90.

W

Wade, Margaret, 150.
Waldman, Louis, 193.
Wales Revival, 25.
Walker, Harry, 194.
Wallace Company, 45.
Wallas, Graham, 86.
Wallin, Samuel, 119, 142-145.
Walton, Frank, 43.
Wanehope, Joseph, 53.
Ward, George W. (Herkimer County Justice),153, 163-164.
Wells, H.G., 95.
Western Federation of Miners, 28-29.
Westinghouse, George Jr, 77.
Whitmyre, H.C., 192.
Williams College, 18.
Williams, John, 135, 139.

Wilson, Woodrow, 31, 34, 47, 50, 84, 85, 89, 141, 143, 147, 154, 187-189, 191.
Wing-Thompson, Dr. Emma, 180.
Winne, Matthew, 43.
Wood, Charles, W., 117, 166.
World War 1, 33-34, 47, 85, 89, 93, 95, 184, 187-188.
Workers International Industrial Union, 29.
Wright, Philip Green, 197.

Y

Yates, Henry R., 169.
Yellow Fever Epidemic of 1867, 27.
YMCA, 21-22.
YWCA, 22.
Yonkers, 9.

Z

Zeidler, Frank, 84.
Zeile, John, 17.
Zugayka, Walter, 152-153.